[JM1] Sp

MW01672158

Toddlers

Develop Early Communication Skills With **137** GAMES Designed by a Speech and Language Therapist

Activities for Pre-School Kids and More!

Kids SLT Publications

A Special GIFT for Every Reader

1. Does your toddler understand basic instructions?
2. Are they able to let you know what they want and need?
3. Do you know how to help your toddler understand your simple instructions?

If you answered 'no' to any or all of the above questions, then you need this **FREE 5-day video training course** is for you.

Simply click the link below – sign up with your email and start receiving one link a day over 5 days.

Follow the strategies and see the progress – let me know how it goes😊

https://www.subscribepage.com/speech-therapy-for-toddlers

Table of Contents

Table of Contents

Introduction **1**

Chapter 1: Why You Should Give a Hoot About OWLING **7**

Getting Down With the Science *7*

What Does Polyvagal Theory Mean for Us? *11*

Porges and OWLING *13*

Chapter 2: What Are Early Interaction Skills and Why Are They So Important **19**

12–24 months *20*

2–3 years *20*

4–6 years *21*

Can I Help My Baby Learn? *22*

Chapter 3: What Can You Do for Your 12–18-Month-Old **24**

The Curiosity Game 26
The Hi and Bye Game 27
The Treasure Path Game 28
The Freeze Game 28
The Fill and Dump Game 28
Name That Body Part Game 29
The Clean Up Game 30
The Build It Break It Game 30
Blowing Bubbles 31
Blowing Feathers 31
Finger Puppet Animals 32

Pretend Play....32
The Sorting Game....33
A Trip to the Park....33
The Funny Faces Game....33
Release the Balloon Game....34
Kisses and Cuddles....34
The One for You One for Me Game....34
The Hokey Cokey/Pokey....35
Water Time....36
If You're Happy and You Know It....36
The Roll the Ball Game....37
Story Time....37
Colouring Time....37
Hygiene and Good Manners....38
Mr Potato Head....39
Make Music....40
Collecting Leaves....40
Build a Ramp....40
Play Skittles....41
Baby Yoga....41

Chapter 4: Fun Games and Techniques to Improve Interaction Skills for 24–36-Month-Olds **43**

Perfect Books for Targeted Speech Sounds....45
Pretend Play Chef....45
Play Hairdressers....46
Teddy Bear's Birthday....47
Emotion Matching Cards....48
Set up a Playdate....48
Sharing Is Caring....49
The Spoons and Foam Game....49
Sock Matching....50
Lily Pad Hop....50
Follow the Leader....51

Puppet Show 51
Dressing Up 52
Ball Time 52
Feed the Monster 53
The Obstacle Course 53
Painting on Unusual Materials 54

Chapter 5: Keeping Your 2½–3-Year-Old Entertained and Learning 55

Perfect Books for Targeted Speech Sounds 57
Pass the Paper, Please 58
Stepping Stones 58
Hide and Seek 59
The Fill the Post Box Game 59
Make a pencil Case 60
Let's Brainstorm 60
The 'What's the Use?' Game 61
I Spy with Colours 62
Simon Says 62
Counting Pasta 63
Sort the Washing 64
Time for Cooking 64
Cupcakes 64
Cheese Biscuits 65
Make a Puzzle 65
3-stage Obstacle Course 65

Chapter 6: From 3–3½ Years – What's Next to Explore? 67

Reinforcing Targeted Speech Sounds 70
Books to Help with Emotions 72
Re-read Stories 72
Remove the Sticky Tape 72
I-Spy Adjectives 73
Making Household Chores a Game 73

Make a Clean-up Tunnel 74
Put the Shopping Away 74
Hunt the Toys in Sand 75
Stone Faces 75
How Many Socks Can You Put On? 76
Screen Time 77
Paint a Picture for a Friend 78
Natural and Related Consequences Matching 78
Happy/Sad Noughts and Crosses/Tic Tac Toe 79

Chapter 7: How Is It Possible That Your Little One Is Nearly 4? What's Next? 80

Perfect Books for Targeted Speech Sounds 83
It's Your Turn 83
The Emotions Thermometer 85
Feelings Charades 85
Draw Your Favourite Song 86
Recycle! 86
Make Your Own Paintbrushes 87
Paint Me 87
Number Stacking 88
We're Going on a Nature Hunt 88
Rice Rainbows 89
Make Yourself Like a 90
Dot to Dots 90
Face Painting 91
Toilet Roll People 91

Chapter 8: Your 4-Year-Old Thinks They Know Best – But You Can Still Help Them to Be Better 93

Perfect Books for Targeted Speech Sounds 96
The Obstacle Course 97
Counting Pasta 97
The Fill the Post Box Game 98

The Staring Game 98
Watch Bluey! 99
My First Map 100
Community Gardening 100
Create a Mini-Me 101
Revise the Chores Chart 102
Family Contest 103
Finish the Story 103
Virtual Playdates 104
Lego Therapy 105
Alphabet Maze 105

Chapter 9: From 4½–5 – The Last Boost Before School 109

Practising Those Blended Sounds 111
Perfect Books for Targeted Speech Sounds 112
The Emotion Thermometer 112
The Marshmallow Test 113
Guess Who 114
The Fill the Post Box Game 115
I Hear With My Little Ear 115
Follow the Grid Game 116
What Should Mummy/Daddy Do? 116
It's Your Turn 118
Developing 'Wh' Questions 118
Sensory Alphabet Hunt 119
Lily Pad Sight Words 120
Puffy Paint 120
Bottle Top Money 121

Chapter 10: Bonus Play Ideas for the Over 5s to Feel More Confident with Friends, Family, and Teachers 123

Perfect Books for Targeted Speech 125
How to Encourage a Love for Reading 126
Word Building 127

Taking Turns in Storytelling 128
Sharing Is Caring 129
Role Play the Harder Things 130
Break out the Board Games 130
Challenge Time 131
Would You Rather 131
After School Activities 132
Anger Drawing 132
Video Games That Help Develop Social Skills 133
Write a Gratitude Letter 134
Make an Art Frame 134
Sofa Time 135

Chapter 11: How to Start Using Social Stories with Children of All Ages **136**

What Are Social Stories? *136*

What's the Difference Between a Social Story and a Comic Strip Conversation? *137*

How to Create Your Own Social Stories *137*

What to Do When You Don't Feel Creative Enough to Write Social Stories *138*

Social Stories and Comic Strip Conversations for Anger *139*
For Toddlers 139
When I Am Calm, Mummy Is Happy 139
For Children 139

15 Social Stories You Can Adapt *142*
First Day of Nursery 142
First Day of School 142
A Visit to the Doctor 143
My First School Trip 143
My Friend Is Autistic 144
My Table Manners 145

Parent's Divorce........ 145
My New Hobby........ 146
My New Sibling........ 146
My First Sleepover........ 147
Going to a Birthday Party........ 147
Taking Turns........ 148
Making Friends........ 148
Potty Training........ 148
Transitioning........ 149

Chapter 12: Walk a Mile in the Parents' Shoes **151**

The Inspirational Julie........ 151

What It's Like Raising a Child With ASD........ 153

Children with Social Anxiety Disorder........ 155

Conclusion **158**

References **165**

Introduction

Just last week I was watching a group of toddlers play as their parents chatted about milestones and how amazing their children were. This is every parent's given right because naturally, their child is the best. But it hurt to watch one mum become quieter and slowly edge away from the group.

When I went over to see if she was ok, I could see just a small tear in her eye and that worried look that we all have when it comes to our little ones. 'What am I doing wrong? My child doesn't say a word and all the books say he should be saying at least 20 words by now!'

All children are going to pick up certain skills faster than others and other talents a little later. Most parents will have that small competitive streak in them, hoping that their child hits the milestones first. But then there are a group of parents who have the most amazing children but struggle to grasp some or all of the social interaction skills that are so crucial to their learning and development.

This is an extremely overwhelming feeling. You want to do everything possible to give them the best start in life, and you worry about bullying, their confidence, or them getting left behind. In a perfect world, healthcare systems would be more on top of this for faster and earlier intervention – however, that's not always the case. It's not always possible to spend much on private therapists and educational toys and games that you know would help.

That doesn't mean to say there is nothing you can do. Before you go rushing off to sign up for parenting classes, child psychology, and child development courses, just take a moment to breathe. Even from where you are sitting now, I am convinced there are everyday items you can use to help improve your child's social interaction skills, whether that's with language development, behavioural issues like turn-taking, or body language such as eye contact.

As a speech and language therapist, I have dedicated my entire career to helping children and their parents work on essential skills involving communication. As a mother of three, I have the added advantage of knowing what parental panic feels like and the constant questioning of whether you are getting things right. Let's address this issue right now: even when your toddler turns 18, you are still going to worry if you are getting it right. It's part of our job.

What you can do is remind yourself that you have done and are doing everything possible to help your child and you are going to become an even better parent after reading this book.

I would be lying if I said I had a passion for writing. As a speech and language therapist, I'm a talker. The reason behind my books is my excitement for sharing knowledge with those people who really need it. After my first book, *Understanding Autism and Speech Therapy for Kids*, I was so moved by hearing from all of you that I knew a simple guide with practical games and ideas would give parents the opportunity to make a difference.

Previously, I looked at specific disorders and delays for concerned parents, whether their children had been diagnosed and they needed to learn more, or if they were just suspicious that their child had a developmental disorder or delay.

Knowing that you are all incredibly busy, I have put together a set of ideas that you can implement with very little to no extra cost. I will go over a range of games and play ideas that will enhance all 10 of the most important early interaction skills for children, including:

- Attention
- Listening
- Play
- Eye contact
- Turn-taking
- Initiating interaction
- Conversational skills
- Following instructions
- Functional language (words to get their needs met)

- Non-verbal communication

Each chapter will focus on a specific age group. Feel free to skip to the chapter that concerns you or read through all of the ideas and adapt them for your child's age. The main age groups will be from 12 months to 5 years, but I wanted to include some additional activities for slightly older children that will also inspire you, for when your little one is a little older.

If you have never heard of social stories, you are in for a treat. Social stories help children of all ages prepare for situations that they have little to no experience of. Think of it as What to Expect when Expecting – but for children and the situations they are about to face. We are going to look at how you can create your own social stories. But for those who have no idea where to begin, you will find a series of stories that you can adapt.

Towards the end of the book, I have leaned on the experiences of some amazing parents as professionals to help put things into perspective and to reassure you that you aren't alone. Furthermore, this chapter highlights just how much you can achieve by spending quality time playing with children at home.

I can't stress this enough – and please forgive me if I repeat this point – but milestones are just a guideline. Toddlers who have been to kindergarten or have lots of other younger children might be better at playing with others than a child who has spent more time with adults only. Manners can depend on cultural differences. Another child can be excellent at following directions but freeze up with their friends. You know your child better than anyone else, so trust your instincts, as you will know what they need.

The reason I emphasize this is because these social skills techniques are supposed to be fun, quality time for you and your child. They are sensitive little people and will pick up on your nerves. So remember, enjoy this precious time with them without any pressure.

We will start with a brief look at the different social skills and how they benefit children – not just now, but when they are older too. We will cover some of the warning signs and what is considered typical behaviour at the different developmental stages, so you have an idea of whether your little one needs professional intervention and/or extra time playing with their favourite people to master these skills. Even if you aren't concerned about your child's social skills, there are still some invaluable ideas for making playtime more enjoyable for the whole family.

Social skills are something that many adults take for granted. We forget that they are not a natural skill we are born with and they are learned. In our first chapter, it's a good moment to make a quick inspection of your own social skills to ensure you are setting the best example.

To do this, we need to go all the way back to our most distant ancestors and explore how our nervous system has evolved and how this has helped scientists and professionals in a wide range of fields to understand social interactions.

Chapter 1: Why You Should Give a Hoot About OWLING

Communication and interaction are a two-way thing. Children learn from their best examples, and that is you as parents. We have had quite a few years to develop our interaction skills but that's not to say we are perfect. And as parents, despite trying our hardest, we know there is room for improvement.

How many times has your child had a meltdown, especially in public, and you have done your best to calm them down? While the judging eyes of your audience stare at your child, the pressure is on for you to resolve this meltdown before you are labelled a terrible parent.

What do we do? Well, anything that we think will help. You might tell your child to look at you in the hope that eye contact means focus. You might give them a hug, attempt a bribe, or put your foot down and not tolerate this behaviour. It's what most of us do and it's what most of our parents did. But there is a better way.

Getting Down With the Science

I have always been a fan of getting down to the science beyond certain topics, especially when related to the body, so that we are better able to understand the why behind our emotions and behaviours. While the nervous system and the brain are extremely complex, I won't get into all the nitty-gritty because as fascinating as it is, it can be overwhelming.

Stephen Porges, professor of psychiatry and a distinguished university scientist, has changed the way both professionals and non-professionals view social interactions with his Polyvagal Theory. The Polyvagal Theory helps us to understand our nervous systems and how they relate to social interactions. Before we look at how his research changed the way we understand the nervous system, let's look at how it was seen before.

Since the beginning of our studies of behaviour, mankind has been described as having two nervous systems. One is the parasympathetic system. This system is active when we feel safe in our social surroundings, and this goes all the way back to cavemen living in social groups. We then have the sympathetic nervous system, often referred to as the fight-or-flight response. When we see danger or a threat, our bodies kick into action and we fight the danger or run. Either way, the danger is removed, and slowly, the body returns to a parasympathetic state.

The chances are, we aren't going to run into a tiger in the wild like our ancestors did, but seeing danger like a dangerous driver or a large figure as you are walking down a dark alley is still going to activate the sympathetic nervous system. But in recent years, the way we categorise the behaviour of humans has significantly evolved.

The Polyvagal Theory states that we don't have two nervous systems but rather, we have three. The first is still our safe, social environment, where our tone of voice and facial expressions reflect our level of comfort. The second is also the fight-or-flight and describes all of our mobile reactions. Porges proposed a third nervous system known as freeze, where we are in an immobile state. This might occur if you arrive home and hear a burglar in your house. You can probably think of some personal experiences where you have been unable to move from fear or shock.

There is a traffic light system that we can use to identify with the three nervous systems:

- **Green:** this is our safe zone. Amazing things happen, like the inner ear getting turned on so we can hear better. Our voices are calm, we can make more eye contact, and our heart rate slows.
- **Yellow:** the heart rate increases, as does the tolerance for pain. Facial expressions become flat and the middle ear switches off so that we are better able to listen to high or low frequencies that warn us of danger.
- **Red:** life-threatening, extreme danger. There is no fight or flight because the nervous system is frozen.

So, in every situation we face, our body starts scanning the environment. The neuroceptions we pick up are feeding the brain with information that activates one of the nervous systems. This is a subconscious action that you can't control but does explain why you instantly like some people but are extremely wary of others – neuroceptions are picking up details that we can't possibly see.

These social cues are often picked up by watching people's faces, the way they smile, and the eye contact they make. But it also includes proximity, the direction people are facing, posture, and crossed arms.

There is a problem with our neuroceptions. Sometimes, we see danger when there isn't a real threat. Those people who have suffered from trauma, or if their sympathetic nervous system is too active, will be biased in certain situations and this leads to the misreading of those situations. Later on, we will discuss trauma because it doesn't necessarily imply a severe event that we associate as traumatic. When this happens, they aren't able to read social cues the same way someone who is in a parasympathetic state will.

For example, a calm, relaxed person may see another person's fidgeting as a sign of them being nervous. A person who is more prone to seeing danger might react to someone else's fidgeting as a sign that this other person feels they are in danger.

What Does Polyvagal Theory Mean for Us?

The Polyvagal Theory helps us to understand so much about communication and behaviour. One excellent example is how different people would act if they were attacked. A very common response is 'Why didn't you run?'. The person likely couldn't run because of the involuntary freeze response. Understanding this alone can help us to empathize with victims, rather than make them feel more like a victim because they didn't run or fight.

Aside from that, the Polyvagal Theory takes us to the very beginning of all communication. By understanding how the nervous systems work, we can be better at helping those who are uncomfortable in social situations. Body language and tone of voice that would otherwise seem aggressive can now be seen as an involuntary act by people to protect themselves and stay safe. This doesn't only apply to other people in social environments but also to yourself. This deeper understanding of your nervous system will help you to understand behaviour, even if you can't pinpoint the root of the emotion.

As a result, we can become more self-aware, more empathetic, and have stronger social connections where both parties feel safe and loved.

Now, at this point, you might be thinking, 'Well, my child hasn't been through any trauma, so how is this relevant?'. Traumatic experiences are not always easy to spot. These tiny little humans pick up on everything, even when we try to protect them from it. Divorce, problems with siblings, or being bullied at school can all cause children to misunderstand social cues and react in a way that doesn't seem appropriate to us.

Every experience we have contributes to who we are as a person, whether we realize it or not. A newborn that has to spend a significant time in hospital will have this experience burnt into their memories, despite not remembering this time. Similarly, if they have an accident or a fall, the experience stays with them. Helicopter parents – those who hover over children – can add to the pressure that a child feels, and while this isn't necessarily traumatic, it's still an experience that is memorized.

It's important not to see these experiences as trauma but simply as an experience that affects the physical or neurological composition of a person, regardless of age. It's also important to understand that you can't blame yourself or feel guilty, especially when you consider that these are experiences that most children will go through, and they could be tiny things that you don't even notice – you aren't with your child 24/7.

Being aware of how your child's nervous system is working will help you to support them in difficult times where social interaction skills seem to be affected.

Porges and OWLING

Today, Stephen Porges continues with his research into mental health. He is the founding director of the Traumatic Stress Research Consortium as well as being a professor of psychiatry. Previously, he had served as the President of the Society for Psychophysiological Research and the Federation of Associations in Behavioral & Brain Sciences. He has published over 300 peer-reviewed papers in a wide range of disciplines and is the recipient of a National Institute of Mental Health Research Scientist Development Award.

More than 1,400 therapists use Porges' music-based intervention to help with spontaneous social engagements, reduce hearing sensitivities, and improve language processing. All of his work is changing the way health professionals look at behavioural, psychiatric, and physical disorders.

Naturally, for me in my specific field, Porges is my hero. His work has helped me to better understand the world of my little clients, as well as that of their parents. After studying his research, I developed OWLING.

OWLING is a concept I have created that will help parents enhance their interactions with children. As much as I would love to go into the details of OWLING, the focus of this book is techniques to play with your little ones. If you would like to learn more about how OWLING can help you and your children, I would love for you to get in touch so I can tell you more about my training programme. You can do so by visiting my website https://kidssltessentials.com/.

The science might feel like a lot to take on when the whole idea is to play and have fun with your child. Nevertheless, with practice, it will become second nature, and rather than jumping in to resolve a problem or initiate play, your observations will teach you more and, consequently, you will both gain from the experience.

I know how difficult it can be to get the right help for your child locally and there is often a long waiting list. For this reason, I would like to briefly introduce you to my training programme, where you can learn about OWLING and much more.

The main goal of the training programme is to provide you with individual, personalized information to help get your little one communicating with their family, friends, teachers, and any other adults they may need to interact with.

The training programme will include teaching workshops plus 1:1 video sessions with you and your child, where we will look at the difficulties your child has and how I can help you to help your child. As well as the OWLING formula, you will learn how to help your child develop their understanding and expressive language, including non-verbal communication skills.

One of the most challenging things as a parent is knowing what to do when your child is suffering from a meltdown. Sometimes, they can completely withdraw from the outside world, while at other times, there could be screaming and legs and arms flapping. You might hear the word 'no' or other words and phrases being repeated, and there may also be repetitive behaviour such as hitting and biting.

This is known as dysregulation and it's basically a way of your child telling you that they are going through a stimulus overload. There is just too much going on for them to cope with. Most parents will try to get involved to try and help, but we actually might just be adding to the stimuli. Another core part of my programme will be understanding the importance of silence and waiting for them to show the signs they are ready to communicate.

Usually what happens in other training courses is that you receive the training online and then you are told to go and implement what you have learnt. When you try things at home with your child, the response from your child might not be as you were trained to expect – what do you do then?! Children will often mimic their parents' reactions and facial expressions and just as often, parents aren't aware of their own expressions and the social cues they are giving their children.

This is the main reason I wanted my training to be different. I have taken the theories of numerous leading professionals, not just Porges, and used them to create a programme that I can teach you, and then we can practice the implementation together.

I want to teach you the strategies and then be there for you when you try them out with your child at home. I will be there to offer alternatives if your child does not respond the way we are expecting them to. I will be there to offer advice, reassurance, and build your confidence as a parent. I will help you to use those intuitive parenting skills you already possess even though you feel you don't know anything – but you do!!

You will have access to the recordings of the workshops if you miss the live sessions. You will be able to download and print the resources. If this sounds like something you would be interested in, then get in touch.

Visit my website https://kidssltessentials.com/ and book a 30-minute FREE consultation with me to see which training program is the most suitable for you. Come and join my Facebook group, which I run for parents of children with delayed speech and language development. This is a great community where you get advice from not only me but other parents around the world and you can share your stories too. There are free resources and best of all, you can get PDF copies of all my books!

https://www.facebook.com/groups/kdslsg.

While I am on the subject, I want to say the biggest thank you to all of the group members. Listening to what you and your children are going through is one of the greatest motivations for this book.

Some of my favourite resources that I have recently made available are a set of journals that can help you to track the progress your children make. Each journal has space for you to track 90 days' worth of progress and yes, they are free. Here are the journals available in my book *Speech Sounds Therapy, A Guide for Parents*:

- Auditory Stimulation strategy to improve your child's clarity of speech

- Listening strategy to improve your child's clarity of speech
- Rhyme and Rhythm strategy to improve your child's clarity of speech
- Speech Sound Awareness strategy to improve your child's clarity of speech
- Syllable Clapping strategy to improve your child's clarity of speech

But for now, let's look at what exactly these interaction skills are and what we should be looking out for during each stage of our children's early years.

Chapter 2: What Are Early Interaction Skills and Why Are They So Important

When parents think about interaction, they will most likely jump straight to those all-important first words. Just for a little giggle: quite a few parents are somewhat taken back when the first word is 'no', even though that is still interaction! In reality, early interaction comes way before these first words.

Early interaction begins as soon as your baby is born. Yes, they can hear you in utero but interaction, by definition, is two-way. It's both verbal and non-verbal communication, such as sounds and actions. When we respond to their sounds and actions, babies learn that their babbling has meaning. From there, they will start interacting with intention, even though words will not have developed yet. The more vocabulary they are exposed to in these early moments, the better prepared they will be for conversing.

During early interactions, young children learn how to initiate interaction with others and respond when someone communicates with them. They get their first experiences with turn-taking and paying attention. As these intentional interactions start to progress, messages become clearer, misunderstandings get resolved by improved communication and new topics are introduced.

Let's take a brief look at what early interaction looks like for different ages.

12–24 months

- Pointing to objects they want
- Raising their hands to be picked up
- Starting to copy/imitate others
- Maintaining eye contact when playing
- Enjoying different toys, textures, colours, and sounds
- Exploring the area around them
- Clapping during social play
- Crawling, climbing, standing, and walking
- Strong and steady enough to play with friends
- Starting to develop group participation
- Enjoying the swings and the playground or being swung in the air
- Able to throw and attempt to catch a ball
- Vocabulary list of around 10 to 20 words
- Developing the sounds /p/, /b/, /m/, /t/, /d/, /n/, and /w/

2–3 years

As well as the above interactions, toddlers will be:

- Interested in playing in small groups
- More aware of eye contact and getting better at maintaining it
- Keen to explore new environments

- Able to play in social situations after a transition time
- Gaining increased coordination to play and explore
- Able to communicate when they are hungry, sad, happy, thirsty, etc.
- Beginning to interact with other adults and able to spend more time away from parents
- Able to sit and listen to a story
- Vocabulary list of approximately 100 words and starting to string together words
- Able to answer simple questions
- Developing the sounds /k/, /g/, /y/, /f/, /s/, and /h/

4–6 years

All of the above skills should be present and it will be a case of continuously working on these skills and adding to them:

- Starting to initiate play with other children
- Possibly showing a preference to playing with friends rather than family
- Playing well in new social situations
- Possibly showing a greater interest in 'rough play' with friends or siblings
- Wide range of vocabulary
- Answering more complex questions that often require reasoning

- Calming themselves down when they are upset
- Developing the cluster sounds /r/, /th/; blended sounds such as /bl/, /cl/, /dr/, /pr/, /tr/, /sp/, /sw/, /spl/, /str/; and the end sound of words like /ls/, /ps/, /ts/, and /vs/

It's always hard creating this type of list because, from a parent's point of view, there is a big difference between a 13-month-old and a 22-month-old. On the other hand, there may only be a day's difference between a three-year-old and a four-year-old. Bear this in mind when you are working through this book.

At the end of each chapter, you will find a checklist with some of the core early interaction skills your little one should have mastered. Bear this in mind when you are working your way through the list. If your child has recently had a birthday, some of these skills won't be present yet.

Can I Help My Baby Learn?

I expect that most readers of this book will have children who are toddlers and older. Nevertheless, you may know someone with a child under one, or if you are thinking of having more, I wanted to add a few ideas that will help parents with babies get off to the best start.

When babies start to coo and gurgle, respond to these sounds. It sounds strange, but wait until they stop making a sound and then take turns. Babies love bright coloured toys that come in different shapes, sizes, and textures. Slowly move different toys so that your baby can follow the object with their eyes. Musical toys are for this as well.

Not only are they more interested in exploring these different toys but you also have more to talk to them about. A wide variety of toys will encourage babies to stretch and hold their heads up during tummy time. The American Academy of Pediatrics recommends starting tummy time as soon as the umbilical cord stump falls off. Just a few minutes at a time, two to three times a day, and always supervised.

Gently clap baby's hands in front of them and stretch their arms slightly. And of course, bring out the child in you by pulling some funny faces for them to learn and soon to start copying.

I know this was quite a short chapter and if you are looking for more specific milestones, you can look at my speech and language development book. The main objective of this book is to provide ideas to increase early interactions. So, let's get started with ways to help your pre-toddler up to two years old. After the 12–24 month period, the differences can be quite a bit bigger in a matter of months. For this reason, from 24 months and upwards, each chapter will look at six months.

Chapter 3: What Can You Do for Your 12–24-Month-Old

Look through the checklist and make notes to see what your child can already do.

Early Interaction Skill	Needs More Work	In Progress	Got It
Shows some interest in toys and pointing to them			
Hands toys to people			
Shakes head to say no			
Vocabulary list of around 10-20 words			
Recognises common, everyday objects			

Shows the beginnings of pretend play (like feeding a stuffed animal)			
Uses a spoon to feed themselves			
Tries to copy others			
Doesn’t notice when the primary caregiver leaves the room			
Follows simple one-step instructions			
Maintaining eye contact when playing			
Able to throw and attempts to catch a ball			

As eager as you are to start playing with your toddler, they may have other intentions. Timing is everything. Make sure that you have eliminated potential stressors like hunger and tiredness. You know what it's like trying to get a toddler dressed when they don't want to – similarly, you can't force them to play!

Toddlers also have short attention spans. You have probably experienced this when you plan the most amazing activity that should keep them happy for an hour or so, only for them to start looking for the next game five minutes later. The general rule of thumb is that a child can concentrate for two to three minutes per year of their age, so realistically, plan for three to five minutes of playtime. If it's more, that's great. But for at least those few minutes, you need to be completely engaged: no mobile, TV, or conversations with other siblings.

Let's start with a few games that promote play and muscle strength. As we move on, you will find different games that promote all 10 aspects of social interaction that we mentioned in the introduction. You can adjust the games to best suit your toddler's age – as we said, the abilities of a 12-month-old aren't the same as those at 24 months.

The Curiosity Game

On a small table, like a coffee table, place different items such as sponges, feathers, a plastic whisk, wooden egg cups, etc. Try to include different colours and textures. At this stage, you will notice little ones pulling themselves up and holding onto the table edge, maybe even moving around the table.

See how they move around to explore the different items. If your child is showing signs of interaction (they are looking at you and making sounds), name the items. If the toddler is older and naming some of the items, try taking one away and saying 'Where is the...?'

This game will help toddlers gain strength as they pull themselves up to stand and balance as they move. You are also introducing new vocabulary.

The Hi and Bye Game

Find a long box and open both ends. While you sit at one end, your toddler sits at the other end. Pop your head into the box and say 'Hello/Hi'. When they put their head in the box to see you, say 'Goodbye/Bye' and move your head out of their sight. Like peek-a-boo, young children find this highly amusing.

This is a good game for children to initiate interaction too. You may find them waving to you from the other side of the box or trying to mimic the words 'hi' and 'bye'. By crawling up to find you, they are also attempting communication.

The Treasure Path Game

Take some of your children's favourite toys and create a path with these toys. The length of the path will depend on their age, but you should try for different heights (that are all safe for them). You might place some on the floor, then a couple on the sofa, back to the floor, and over a small coffee table[JM2].

As well as working on their muscle strength and balance, your little one will be communicating with you by their facial expressions. You might be able to see if they are frustrated when they can't reach something, or ecstatic when they stand up and discover their favourite toy on a table.

The Freeze Game

You can play this game with music or as you are singing along to nursery rhymes. When the music or song stops, they have to freeze. This is a very simple game that helps little ones with their listening and attention skills as well as self-regulation, controlling their actions. It's a very good way for toddlers to follow instructions, which they will need at nursery or school.

The Fill and Dump Game

There are different variations to this game. First, you can make your own balls from things like scrunched-up newspaper, or use plastic balls if you have them. Fill one shoebox with the balls and have another one close by. If they are walking or crawling, put the boxes a little further apart to encourage movement.

Sit down opposite each other with the boxes in between you. Show them how to pick up one ball and put it in the empty box. When making eye contact, tell them it's their turn, then your turn, and so on.

If they are older, you can have different coloured balls and ask them to move a specific-coloured ball. You can also ask them which colour you should move next. Other variations include loud and quiet objects.

You might not realise this, but the action of moving their hand across their body when moving the balls is essential for various skills later on in life, one of which is writing. (You aren't alone if you are moving an imaginary ball across your body now!)

Name That Body Part Game

This game can be played during dedicated playtime or when they are getting dressed or in the bath. Point to different parts of the body, touch, or lift up parts; make sure it is clear which body part you are indicating. Say, 'What's this?' and respond, 'It's your foot.' Repetition is crucial because the more you play this game, the more vocabulary they will learn.

You can also sit your toddler in front of you and say things like 'Where is my mouth?' and have them point to your mouth. Or 'Where is your mouth?' so that they point to theirs. It won't be long until they are trying to copy the words.

The Clean Up Game

Though not on the list of early interaction skills, it is still important to teach young children how to take care of and be responsible for their own things. One way to do this is to clean up together. You can sing, 'Clean up, clean up, everybody let's clean up'. You can have a race to see who can pick up the most toys.

If you ask your child to pick up different toys to put away, it will improve their listening and attention skills. They might say the names of things for you to put away or point to, which is not just initiating interaction but is also turn-taking. Not to mention, you aren't left putting away all the toys – again!

The Build It Break It Game

Blocks are great fun for toddlers and it's great to watch the look of concentration on their faces. Stacking blocks gives you a chance to take turns and build vocabulary such as colours and counting. Name the colours of the blocks as they stack them, and ask them to put different coloured blocks on next. Every time someone adds a block, count how many there are. When you have finished, let them knock over their stack of blocks: it's the first stage of learning cause and effect.

Blowing Bubbles

It's hard to meet a toddler who doesn't love this inexpensive game. You can obviously buy bubbles, or you can make them at home. Rather than just washing up liquid and water, add some corn syrup or sugar for better bubbles. Don't forget you can rub a little body gel into your hands and use your thumb and index finger to blow bubbles in the bath, though this will be tricky for a toddler to copy.

When children blow bubbles, they are controlling inhalation and exhalation. This is essential for speech and language development because it is how different sounds are produced. What's more, when toddlers pop bubbles with their fingers, they are working on hand-eye coordination.

Blowing Feathers

Another idea to help with breathing control is to blow feathers. If you have a jungle gym, you can tie different coloured feathers from string, or you can use an umbrella and enjoy some outdoor time. Younger toddlers will enjoy reaching out to touch the different feathers, and you can ask older toddlers to blow a certain colour.

Finger Puppet Animals

Finger puppets can be made out of old socks: draw animal faces on them, or use yellow rubber gloves, which make excellent ducks. With animal finger puppets, toddlers can start practising animal sounds and names. It is also a good way to introduce pretend play, but you also get the chance to start showing toddlers the importance of taking turns in conversations.

Pretend Play

Pretend play is an opportunity for children to act out and even practise different social situations. It's an all-round activity that helps practise vocabulary, understand emotions, problem-solving, and self-regulation. Of course, at this stage, pretend play will be limited, but as they get closer to the 24-month stage, they will show more interest.

Pretend play might start off with finger puppets, hand puppets, dolls, or special toy characters they love. When your child offers you a toy, use this toy to say 'Hello' to the toy they have. Wait for your child to initiate interaction, even if this is just a sound in response to your hello. Much like with their early babbling, toddlers soon learn how to take turns with pretend play conversation.

The Sorting Game

Again, there are many different ways that you can play this type of game. You can take four different coloured pieces of paper and put them on the floor. Toddlers can sort out coloured hair scrunchies, pieces of Play-Doh, or straws. You could have different pots and sort out different pasta shapes.

Sorting games help young children to notice similarities and differences. While they are paying attention to the sorting, they will also be problem-solving and categorising, which will help with numeracy skills later on.

A Trip to the Park

Fresh air, physical activity, and the chance to explore new surroundings and build confidence. If your toddler isn't socialising with others yet, the park is an ideal place for them to meet new friends and begin interacting with other children. While your child is interacting with other children, you have the perfect opportunity to observe.

The Funny Faces Game

If you want to encourage eye contact, funny faces will encourage your children to remain focused on your face. You can add funny glasses or different hats to make the game more exciting. You can incorporate turn-taking by giving your toddler a hat and saying, 'Your turn.' You can also copy their facial expressions so that they begin to copy yours.

Release the Balloon Game

Like bubbles, balloons are a favourite for many children. Inflate a balloon, when your child makes eye contact with you, let go of the balloon and both of you can try and catch it. Be sure not to leave balloons around while you aren't there because they could be a choking hazard.

Kisses and Cuddles

Though not essentially a game, kisses and cuddles serve multiple purposes. First, it's a chance for physical contact to show each other love. Next, cuddles help your child to feel safe and secure, which will help them feel more confident in other social environments. Finally, there are lots of kisses you can give, and all will help with eye contact. Have a go at Eskimo kisses where you rub noses, and butterfly kisses where you brush your eyelashes up and down their cheek as you blink.

The One for You One for Me Game

The concept of sharing isn't normally understood until the age of three, but you can still begin this important play skill with toddlers, and it can be done with different activities throughout the day. One toy for you, one toy for me, one crayon for you, one crayon for me, and so on. When your child starts copying and giving you objects, make sure there is lots of praise to encourage them to keep up the good sharing.

The Hokey Cokey/Pokey

Just in case you can't remember this one...

You put your left arm in
Your left arm out
In, out, in, out
You shake it all about
You do the hokey cokey
And you turn around
That's what it's all about

Woah, the hokey cokey
Woah, the hokey cokey
Woah the hokey cokey
Knees bent
Arms stretched
Ra-ra-ra

Now, if you are anything like me, you might have a few issues with your own left and right, so it's not like you have to expect a toddler to get this concept. But, even when they are younger, you can sing this song and move their body parts for them. As they start to get older, toddlers will copy your movements. The hokey cokey is a great game for young children to listen and follow directions.

Water Time

It's time to get a little wet but have lots of fun. Playing with a simple bucket of water has no end of options. There is pouring water into different sized containers, adding their favourite plastic toys, giving dolls a bath and pretend play, or even just splashing.

Playing with water helps with concentration; it's easier for children to pay attention to a play activity that they enjoy. It can develop gross and fine motor skills as well as hand-eye coordination. There are also mathematical concepts that can be introduced, relating to volume and weight. When children are happily engaged in an activity, they are more inclined to communicate with you, as they want you to join in.

If You're Happy and You Know It

The first set normally starts with 'If you're happy and you know it, clap your hands'. But with a little bit of creativity, you can add your own emotions and different actions. For example, 'If you're tired and you know it, stretch your arms' or 'If you're angry and you know it, honk your nose'.

What are the benefits of this 1950s song? Children are recognising emotions and learning that it's ok to express these feelings rather than ignore these feelings. There is then the advantage of listening for instructions and following those instructions.

The Roll the Ball Game

You can play this game with your toddler or encourage siblings to join in too. Sit on the floor with your legs open, and ask the children to do the same. Say the child's name, when and only when they look at you and make eye contact, and then you roll the ball to them. Aside from coordination, toddlers are learning about turn-taking and listening skills.

Story Time

Books open children's minds and imaginations. They are introduced to new vocabulary, sounds, stress patterns, and inspiration for pretend play. Young toddlers will enjoy listening to you making different voices for characters, and older toddlers can be asked to point to different objects and name the colours. Encourage engagement with books about their favourite characters, as well as books that contain hidden flaps and textures.

Colouring Time

It's early days for colouring and scribbling but at this age, they are still able to improve hand strength and pencil grip. Colouring lets children express themselves and encourages creativity. It's an activity that can hold children's attention for longer than others, especially if they have a wide range of non-toxic colouring tools.

I find that colouring with toddlers is the perfect time to emphasize good manners. Throughout everyday activities, you are probably paying more attention to 'please' and 'thank you'. When you and your toddler are colouring together, ask questions like 'Can you pass me the yellow crayon please,' and don't forget to model the correct behaviour with a 'Thank you'.

I fully understand that 'please' and 'thank you' are different from one culture and language to the next. One English mum who lives in Spain told me that 'please' tended to be implied in the tone of voice there, but it was hard for her when people never said 'Please' or 'Thank you', added to which she was not able to detect it in the tone of voice. I'm not suggesting that everyone should follow English culture – far from it. However, do get used to the customs of the culture and country you live in because this is where your child's social interactions are going to take place.

Hygiene and Good Manners

More than ever, the thought of someone coughing without covering their mouth is going to upset you. Little people aren't aware of how quickly germs can spread from coughing, but part of having good manners is to teach this type of thing. While we should be coughing into a tissue, we don't always have one at hand for ourselves, let alone our toddlers.

Most of us are used to shouting 'Hand!' every 30 seconds when children aren't well. But the hand is not recommended and if we can make a game out of this, you will find it more effective. Try things like the Superhero V, the V being the shape created in your elbow when you bend your arm. You can make it any type of V that will motivate your toddler, for example, Princess V or Ninja V. Whatever V you choose, say it when they cough or sneeze to remind them to cover their mouth.

Mr Potato Head

You don't need to have the actual Mr Potato Head toy. You can draw or print a picture, stick it on some card, and laminate it to last longer. Do the same with the different parts of the body. Mr/Mrs Potato Head is fantastic for functional language like 'Put the hat on his head' and 'Put the eyes in the head'. You can put parts of the body in the wrong place and ask, 'Does the mouth go here?' You might start by putting the mouth in a few incorrect places before you get the right one and they say 'Yes'. Or they might initiate interaction by taking the body part and putting it in the right place.

Make Music

Studies show that having music sessions with parents at as young as one year old can lead to more smiling, less emotional distress when things don't go their way, more pointing, and better communication (Science Daily, 2012). Again, there is no need to go out and buy musical instruments. Turn your saucepans upside down and give them a wooden spoon to bang away to their heart's content. Fill up bottles with different dried items that they can shake and rattle. Place elastic bands over different hollow materials for them to pluck.

Collecting Leaves

I love being able to get outside with little ones as often as possible. Autumn is a great time to watch the leaves falling from the trees. Toddlers can enjoy playing in the dry leaves. If you take a box or bucket, your little one can collect leaves. You can use functional language like 'big' and 'small' and improve fine motor skills with the pinching action to pick up leaves. As a bonus, take the dry leaves home, place them under a piece of paper, and colour over them.

Build a Ramp

You most likely have a box or some packaging that can be opened up and placed so one end is resting on a chair or low table. Use this ramp for your child to roll objects down. It requires a certain amount of attention for an object to roll all the way down the ramp. Choose different objects to see which ones are fast and which ones are slow. Extend the game by taking turns. If you feel your child needs help with eye contact, make sure you sit so that your eyes are level with the top of the ramp.

Play Skittles

Skittles is a game that has more gross and fine motor skill benefits than social interaction skills, but don't forget the importance of having fun; rolling a pair of socks into a ball and attempting to knock over empty plastic bottles is a game where your toddlers will enjoy watching you have fun. Make sure you stick to the rule of one turn each and encourage your child to help stand the bottles up again.

Baby Yoga

Signing up for a toddler yoga class is an excellent way to bond and meet other young children. Yoga is a chance for your little one to relax and focus on their breathing. Yoga also provides them with new vocabulary like 'up', 'down', 'left', and 'right'. They also need to follow instructions. If you don't have any local classes, have a look for Cosmic Kids on YouTube.

They have different stories, such as We're Going On a Bear Hunt, combined with yoga.

Chapter 4: Fun Games and Techniques to Improve Interaction Skills for 24–36-Month-Olds

Look through the checklist and make notes to see what your child can already do.

Early Interaction Skill	Needs More Work	In Progress	Got It
Has a vocabulary of at least 50 words			
Begins to string two or three words together			
Follows two-step instructions			
Understands the concept of turn-taking			

Shows a wide range of emotions			
Enjoys playing with other children			
Is able to sort objects by shape/colour/size			
Is comfortable making eye contact			
Can sit and listen to a story			
Can answer simple questions			

It's this six-month period in which we start to realise our little babies are no longer babies. They will be steadier on their feet and getting more confident when trying things like running and jumping. More sounds are being replaced with words, even if they aren't completely understandable.

After the second birthday, children start to develop their own dependence, and with this comes the magic word 'no'. On the other hand, they still can't resist the chance to play with you. Let's start with some ideas to develop those key speech sounds.

Perfect Books for Targeted Speech Sounds

Children at this age should have a strong grasp of the sounds /p/, /b/, /m/, /t/, /d/, and /w/. These are the foundation sounds of our language. If they haven't quite mastered them, you can't move onto the next stage, or else you will end up with a rather wobbly house. The following books are perfect to help your little one practise these sounds:

- *Wendy's Winter Walk*
- *Brown Bear, Brown Bear, What Do You See?*
- *Pizza Pat*
- *The Wheels on the Bus*
- *If You Give a Moose a Muffin*
- *Barnyard Dance*
- *Teeny Tiny*
- *How Many Bugs in a Box*

Pretend Play Chef

Pretend play gives your little one to explore their imagination and creativity. It actually gives you the chance to observe while they are making their creations, and it is your time to see just how much vocabulary they have.

Using homemade Play-Doh and some of your own baking utensils, like a rolling pin and a plastic knife, ask them if they would like to make you a pizza. If it's not a pizza, ask them what food they would like to make. As well as the vocabulary you can introduce, you can start with sequencing: 'first, we roll out the dough, next, we add the tomato sauce,' etc.

Play Hairdressers

Please don't think this is just an activity for girls! At this age, you may notice that your child goes through a hair-pulling, hitting, or biting phase. Despite being very compassionate, they are not always aware of the pain that this can cause.

Personally, I find someone playing with my hair very relaxing, so much so I am often tempted to bribe my teenage girls just so they sit and brush my hair. Still, when they were 25/26 months old, I was less keen.

Giving your little one the hairbrush and letting them brush your hair improves hand-eye coordination. It teaches them about personal care and makes it easier when it comes to you doing their hair. Most importantly, it gives them a chance to learn what to do when they hurt someone.

Where possible, let them see how you brush someone else's hair. Let the other person know that you need a pretend 'ow' every now and then. Say 'Sorry' to your volunteer and give them a kiss where you hurt them. This is the model behaviour your little one will love to copy.

Teddy Bear's Birthday

It doesn't have to be a birthday, it can be a tea party, superhero, or princess dinner party, a sticker swapping party, or anything that gets your child excited. This is another pretend play activity that I use to help work on emotional understanding. Remember that jumping straight in with questions like 'Why is Teddy angry?' is unlikely to get a response like, 'Well Mum, his best friend couldn't come so now Teddy is angry.'

It is best to ask simple questions like 'Is Teddy happy?' or 'Is Teddy sad?'. If they say 'Yes' or 'No', you could follow up with 'Is Teddy happy because he likes the cake?' or if Teddy is sad, you can make suggestions to see how Teddy could be happier.

Children need to learn that it's ok to have different emotions rather than being told that only positive emotions are good. This will help them with their own emotion management and to be more empathetic towards their peers later on.

Emotion Matching Cards

Another way to actively encourage young children to talk about different emotions is to print two sets of different emotions or draw them if you want. Stick them on a piece of card and laminate them if you want them to last longer. Emotions to include are 'happy', 'sad', 'excited', 'surprised', 'scared', and 'angry'.

Along with emotional awareness, matching pictures promotes attention and helps with problem-solving skills. You can also take turns in pairing up the emotion cards.

Set up a Playdate

Playdates are the ideal way to start watching your little one interacting with others. Children don't necessarily have to be exactly the same age. If there is a few months' difference, they will still be able to play together well. At this stage, they will understand that there is a difference between boys and girls but that shouldn't influence who you invite.

As your little one plays with their new friend, resist the urge to get involved unless necessary. Observe, listen to them, see if there are certain toys that they like to show their friend. Do they come across as confident or shy? From here, you can look at other games that will build the skills they need.

Sharing Is Caring

Another favourite word that appears is 'mine'. It's true that everything from their crayons to your laptop seems to be theirs, but this is the perfect time to teach young children that even if something is theirs, they can still let someone else use it and it will be returned.

This is another time for model behaviour but there are of course limits. You aren't going to let your two-year-old on your computer or to really use your phone. However, there are things that you can share, even if it's something simple like your pen. Set a timer so they know that there is a time limit and after that, they have to give your item back. Make sure they are aware of the timer and what has to happen when the time runs out.

The Spoons and Foam Game

First of all, don't leave your child unsupervised, in case they take a mouthful of shaving cream. Also, it's a good idea not to use the usual spoon they eat with because naturally, they are going to associate the spoon with eating.

Get two big bowls (preferably plastic). Fill one up with shaving foam. Show your child how to scoop the shaving foam from one bowl to the other. If you want to use different smaller bowls, you can add drops of food colouring so that they can mix colours together in the big bowl. Shaving foam is a good material for children to practise using a spoon, which will help them with learning to eat independently.

Sock Matching

Due to the mysterious sock-eating washing machine, it's rare to meet a parent who likes matching socks. Children, on the other hand, seem to love it. Matching socks gives them the chance to focus on the shapes, colours, patterns, and size of the socks. This is all vocabulary that may or may not be used but can be practised. You can add new vocabulary like 'soft' and even point out what a hole is (or maybe that's just my house!).

Lily Pad Hop

By cutting out big lily pads and sticking them on the ground, your child can jump from one to another – and they can make frog sounds if they want to. You can make this more challenging by adding some blue circles for them not to jump on, improving their attention and concentration.

This game is going to develop their leg muscles and help them with balance but it will also start to teach them about spatial awareness. Spatial awareness is essential in social situations because it helps us to recognise and respect other people's personal space.

Follow the Leader

Follow the Leader can be played indoors or out, with or without siblings, and it is a nice way to have five minutes (or more) of active time. You can start off with simple actions like walking and then you can add things like 'Touch your toes', 'Hands in the air', 'Jump up and down', and so on. After you have been the leader, let your little one have a go too.

Aside from the physical activity and development, children are also learning how to follow instructions. When they are the leader, they have a chance to build confidence. Although they might not give full instructions, they will be able to practise saying words they are familiar with like 'walk', 'run', 'sit', 'jump', and 'stop'.

Puppet Show

Prior to their second birthday, you may have been a one-parent puppet show, playing the parts of all characters. Now that they are slightly older, you can ask if they would like to have a puppet for their finger or fingers.

Let your child lead with the story that is created for the puppets. They might take a toy car and pretend that the puppet is going for a drive. Or they might want to add toy animals to their story. Your puppets are the supporting actors rather than the star! By letting them lead, they will be gaining confidence, expressing their emotions, and reading yours when you respond.

Dressing Up

This is an interesting game to watch in terms of copying the behaviour and emotions of others. Give your child a box of different clothes to try on. This might be some dress-up clothes they have of their favourite characters, or you could add some older siblings' clothes and your own.

Dressing up sparks their imagination. It gives children the chance to take on another persona. Studies have shown that both children and older adults perform better in tackling challenging tasks when they take on a persona. This is known as the Batman Effect. It's worth paying attention to see if your little one appears more confident when they are dressing up, and seeing if they copy the behaviour of the person they are dressed up as.

Ball Time

You can take different-sized balls and leave a box on its side and another one upright. This way, they have the option to kick the various balls into a box or throw them. Move the boxes every once in a while.

Playing with balls helps with coordination. But when you add different-sized balls, children will learn how different weights require different forces and that the amount of force will change for different distances.

Feed the Monster

Take a paper bag and cut a mouth on one side. You can also draw a monster face to go with the mouth. Take different items, preferably things that they know the names of. Tell your child that the monster is hungry and that they need to feed it. Use sentences like 'Can you feed the monster the ball?' so that they are following instructions. You could also ask them what they would like to feed the monster, so that they are saying the words of the items. You can keep feeding the monster until it is full or tips over.

The Obstacle Course

This is another idea that can be done inside or outside, depending on what materials you have available. It goes without saying that the course you create has to be safe. You can lay some rope on the ground for them to walk along, chairs to crawl under, and substitute cones to weave in and out of.

You have physical benefits such as strength and balance. On the other hand, children are developing their spatial awareness skills, they are listening and paying attention to your instructions.

Painting on Unusual Materials

Painting is a good messy time activity, one that revises colours while inspiring creativity. You can of course use body parts like fingers, hands, and feet if you are feeling brave. Or you can paint on unusual materials like crushed ice or ice cubes. This sparks a curiosity in little ones and doubles up as a sensory activity.

At this point, I would like to remind you that the games listed in the previous chapter are still relevant for this age group. For example, if you are a fan of yoga, you will know just how much you benefit from it, so it's an activity for all ages. The other games can be adapted and made more challenging for 24-to-36-month-olds.

The same can be said for the next chapter. Please feel free to adapt any game, depending on the needs of your little one.

Chapter 5: Keeping Your 2½–3-Year-Old Entertained and Learning

Look through the checklist and make notes to see what your child can already do.

Early Interaction Skill	Needs More Work	In Progress	Got It
Has a vocabulary of between 100 and 150 words			
Is developing the sounds /k/, /g/, /y/, /f/, and /h/			
Is more comfortable being away from primary caregiver and spending time with other adults			

Stacks blocks, copying another stack of blocks			
Holds pencils/crayons and shows an interest in colouring			
Can complete simple puzzles			
Can kick a ball and attempt to throw a ball			
Understands the concept of 'mine' and 'yours'			
Shows more interest in pretend play with things like finger puppets			

Begins to answer 'wh' questions			

One of the main things you will notice around this time is how short sentences start forming. Rather than just words, you will notice that you may have some three or four-word sentences. This makes communication all the more fun. Be sure not to laugh at your little ones as they begin to form these sentences. We do this because they are just so adorably cute and not because we are laughing at them, but we don't want to risk hurting their confidence.

If you haven't already started, it is probably time for potty training. This is a huge milestone and one that will fill your little one with confidence, making them feel like a big girl/boy. Accept that there will be more washing in this phase and never get angry. It will help to use stories and songs to help.

Let's look at some games that will continue to spark an interest and develop those all-important social skills at this age.

Perfect Books for Targeted Speech Sounds

The targeted sounds in this age group are /k/, /g/, /y/, /f/, /s/, and /h/. Here are just a few examples of books that will encourage the right speech sound development:

- *A Fish Out of Water*
- *Go, Dog, Go*
- *Some Smug Slug*
- *Horace and Morris Say Cheese*
- *Polar Bear, Polar Bear, What Do You Hear?*
- *Good Night, Gorilla*
- *I Feel a Foot*
- *Clifford, the Big Red Dog*

Pass the Paper, Please

You may as well get used to your children following you into the bathroom – it's like some kind of universal rule for them. Nevertheless, you can take advantage of this time by helping your child become familiar with items in the bathroom. As they get more comfortable in the bathroom, it will be easier for them to go to the potty. Ask them if they can help you to tear off the paper or press the flush for you. Then you can wash your hands together. Establishing this routine as early as possible makes the process easier.

Stepping Stones

As a step up from the Lily Pad game, you can make a stepping stones game. Now you can make the paper stones smaller, definitely with different colours and maybe even some simple shapes. Space the paper stones out so that your child has to make an effort to reach the next one but not so they have to jump.

This activity reinforces colours and shapes but above all, it promotes listening and following instructions. If there is an older sibling, they may want to get involved so that they are both taking turns.

Hide and Seek

Bear in mind the attention span for children of this age is still going to be relatively short. Hiding under a blanket is a little too easy but hiding in a wardrobe might be too extreme. It's possible they will get bored and leave you there! If they haven't quite got to counting to 10, they can count to 5, but get them to touch their toes between each number so you have time to hide.

You can give your little one some clues by making a noise or calling their name. This will improve their listening skills and problem-solving skills.

The Fill the Post Box Game

Take an old box, cut a slot in it, and decorate it like a post box – you can do this together. Next, make cards with different items on them. It could be food, animals, toys, even photos of family members. To make the game last longer, laminate them. Take the cards and hide them around the room. Ask them to find the different cards and post them in the box.

Introduce the concept of warmer when they get close and colder as they move further away. If they discover another card, remind them of the image they are supposed to be looking for. There are a number of benefits to this game, from vocabulary to attention, and even fine motor skills when posting the images.

Make a pencil Case

Sometimes, it's perfectly ok to just do something creative without having a social interaction skill in mind. For example, making a pencil case together is a great way for the two of you to bond, have fun, and naturally use some of the skills you have been working on, like 'Please' and 'Thank you', and sharing the materials.

Take a small box and either paint it or cover it with paper. Then together, you can use colours, stickers, or glitter if you are feeling brave, to decorate the pencil case.

Aside from imagination and creativity, this teaches your child that they need to take care of their own belongings and that they should be responsible for these things. This will be a valuable lesson for when they start school.

Let's Brainstorm

Now, this is a good one for developing those early interaction skills. This is a good age for children to learn that not everything will go the way they want. It's perfectly normal for young children to be faced with a problem, not know how to solve it, and end up having a tantrum.

When children are faced with a problem, it's incredibly useful to sit down with them and talk about the different solutions. For example, if their sibling doesn't want to play with them, it's not fair to force the sibling just to prevent a tantrum. Instead, you and your little one could talk about activities they could do alone or games that they can play with you and maybe later, when their sibling has finished their activities, you can suggest a fun activity for both of them. This is the perfect time to introduce the 'Now and Then' strategy.

That's not to say you are going to eliminate all tantrums. But you will start showing your child how to problem solve and to see things from other people's points of view, which will encourage empathy. Of course, they will also start to see the benefits of compromise.

The 'What's the Use?' Game

You can play this game during dedicated playtime or as you are going about your everyday tasks. Take some typical objects that they use, like shoes, spoons, a sponge, and so on. Ask them what they use them for, so: 'What do you use a spoon for?'. You may also ask things like 'Where do we put our shoes?'. At this age, they are starting to respond to 'what' and 'where' questions and this game will encourage them to make their own simple questions.

I Spy with Colours

The traditional 'I spy with my little eye something beginning with…' followed by a letter is obviously not practical at this age as their literacy skills aren't quite there. Nevertheless, I Spy is a great game to keep children entertained and you also have the chance to revise key vocabulary. Try to choose a colour that has various visible objects – that way, they can really put their observational skills to use.

Be sure to repeat the phrase 'I spy with my little eye something that is the colour…' as they will learn from this repetition. Even if they begin with 'I spy blue', they are still understanding the concept of the game and practising turn-taking.

Simon Says

It's a classic game and although the rules are simple, you know how easy it is to get wrapped up in the game and not listen out for 'Simon says'. Begin with simple actions like 'touch your nose' or 'clap your hands'. Emphasize the words 'Simon says' to show the importance of these two words. Perform the actions with them and when you don't say 'Simon says', don't perform the action, at least in the beginning while they are getting the hang of it.

If they perform the action without 'Simon says', it is then their turn. It's important to stick to the rules because otherwise, when they are playing with their friends, they won't appreciate how rules apply to everyone. Depending on their language development, for their turn, they might say a complete sentence: 'Simon says clap your hands' or perhaps 'Simon says clap'. Make sure you are using complete instructions for them to follow so they can learn.

Counting Pasta

We need to provide as many opportunities for young children to practise their counting skills as possible. This can be very simple; you can count the cars you see or the flowers in the garden. When you are shopping, you can count the number of apples or oranges you put in a bag.

To count pasta, take different sized Tupperware pots. Ask them to put, for example, 5 pieces of pasta in one pot, 7 in another, 10 or 12 in a different pot. You can also have them count the pasta as they take the pieces back out. Of course, pasta is just one idea. You can use any item but I wouldn't recommend chocolate – you might find it's one for the pot and one for the mouth!

Sort the Washing

This works for when you are hanging the washing out or putting clean washing away. When you have your washing basket, ask them to pass you different items. I would advise you to hang out the larger items first as they could end up on the floor. Rather than just asking for a sock, ask for Mum or Dad's sock. This gives them the chance to listen for specific vocabulary. At the same time, they are taking part in family chores and learning that it's the responsibility of everyone, not just the adults.

Time for Cooking

It's messy, but that's life. When your little one sees their creation coming out of the oven, the smile and pride will be worth a bit of extra cleaning. Cooking is the perfect time to show young children the importance of measuring your ingredients: they can use a spoon to help you measure and you can teach them the number you are looking for on the scales. Do this in single digits like '1, 1, 0' instead of '110'. Either let them or help them pour the ingredients into the bowl and take turns in mixing. Here are two simple recipes that are great for little ones.

Cupcakes

150g of self-raising flour, 150g margarine, 150g of sugar, 3 eggs, vanilla. Mix all of the ingredients together and put the mixture into cupcake papers. Cook at 180°C for approximately 20 minutes. Once they have cooled, you can decorate them with sprinkles or melted chocolate.

Cheese Biscuits

225g self-raising flour, 110g of margarine, 110g of grated cheese, 1 egg, 1 egg yolk. Mix all the ingredients, wrap in cling film and leave to chill in the fridge for half an hour. Roll the dough out to about 2cm thick and use cookie cutters to make the biscuits. Cook in the oven at 180°C for around 15 minutes.

Make a Puzzle

Puzzles are good for finger strength and hand-eye coordination. They also have the advantage of encouraging problem-solving and perseverance. The great thing is that you can make your own puzzles from photos to help them feel more engaged and it gives you more to talk about. You can even choose photos of things they did in the past to include concepts of time and those all-important past-tense verbs.

3-stage Obstacle Course

If possible, use this as an outdoor activity. At this age, children love to pedal on tricycles or bicycles, so it's a good activity to add to your obstacle course. Children at this age will probably be able to follow three or four instructions. So, create three or four activities, give them the instructions at the beginning and see if they can remember the correct order of the obstacle course. Once they have mastered it a few times, change the order of the tasks and give them new instructions.

Chapter 6: From 3–3½ Years – What's Next to Explore?

Look through the checklist and make notes to see what your child can already do.

Early Interaction Skill	Needs More Work	In Progress	Got It
Speaks more than 250 words			
Strings four to five words together in simple sentences			
Has speech that is clear to those who are close			
Recognises and names objects in a book			

Remembers stories and the names of favourite books			
Understands and has begun counting			
Is beginning to enjoy playing with groups of children			
Is starting to show more complex emotions such as guilt, envy, and empathy			
Recognises about half the letters of the alphabet			
Performs more realistic pretend play (treating toys as if they were alive)			

All sorts of crazy things start happening at this age, some amazing, others not so. Typically, this is the time when toddlers start nursery or preschool. Just take a moment to think about how you feel on the first day of a new job. Now consider how advanced your social skills are compared to your three-year-old's!

It's exciting for them. All of a sudden, they have multiple other children to play with, toys they have never seen, and adults they have never interacted with. At the same time, they don't have the same contact with their usual caregiver. This new routine is a little bit exhausting.

Generally speaking, once settled into their new routine, their social interaction skills will develop quite rapidly at this stage because they are around so many other children. But Mother Nature has a wonderful trick to keep us parents on our toes.

Regression! Have you ever noticed how everything seems to be going in the right direction and then all of a sudden, your toddler stops advancing and even seems to go backwards in their development? They might have been potty trained for months but then start having accidents. They may have been sleeping through the night and now it feels like you are back to newborn night times.

Some of the most common regressions are with sleeping, but it can also occur with eating habits, language, asking for their dummy, and so on.

Regression will also occur at different stages of their early lives.

Children may regress when they feel overwhelmed about situations going on. By regressing back to an earlier stage of their lives, children are able to find comfort. Although it can happen at any age, I wanted to mention this now, because starting nursery is such a massive change for them that regression may occur.

Parents shouldn't panic too soon. Regression normally lasts for a few weeks and you can probably shorten this period if you are able to pinpoint what is causing their upset. Regression is a temporary state, so you shouldn't be confused by a delay or disorder in their early interaction skills. If it does feel like this period of time is lasting too long, then you can take it up with your doctor.

A good idea to help comfort your little one is to go back to some of their favourite games, stories, and activities such as those mentioned in the previous chapters. Sometimes, familiarity can be very reassuring.

Reinforcing Targeted Speech Sounds

Typically at this age, children will still be developing the sounds I have covered previously. If you see that they haven't quite got these sounds yet, here are some ideas to help them.

- /b/, /p/ – start by teaching them how to press their lips together and gently force the air out as they make their lips pop. Show them how by doing it yourself. When they master this action, encourage them to add a big voice for /b/ and a small voice for /p/.
- Take some bubble wrap and each time you pop a bubble, say 'Pop!'. Take a ball and on every bounce, say the b sound.
- /m/ – humming helps to develop the /m/ sound. Begin by taking some of your child's favourite nursery rhymes and hum them together.
- /t/, /d/ – sometimes children struggle with the t sound because they can't find the right spot where their tongue should be. First, identify this spot in your mouth so you can show them. Touch this area in their mouth with a popsicle stick. You can use the stick to put some food there and have them lick it off. The /d/ sound is the same process but they will need to use their big voice to produce the sound.
- /n/ – the tongue has to find the same spot as the /d/ and /t/ and then combine this with an open-mouthed hum. Take chopsticks and pretend to be music conductors with the sounds: 'na naaa, na naa'.
- /w/ – say a word that starts with 'w' and notice how the shape of your mouth is similar to the shape you make with a kiss. Give each other

lots of kisses and exaggerate the 'ooouuh' sound as you kiss.

Books to Help with Emotions

Emotional awareness is essential at this stage as they may now be taking in the emotions of other children. Some excellent stories to help little people to start naming some of their more challenging emotions include:

- *One of Those Days*
- *The Pigeon Has Feelings Too!*
- *The Feelings Book*
- *Glad Monster, Sad Monster*
- *The Way I Feel*
- *The Way I Feel Series* by Cornelia Maude Spelman

Re-read Stories

Have you noticed how you can read a story so many times that when you are driving with your children, you can retell the whole book? That's not to say that you should abandon these books because there is still a lot of joy to be had. What you can do is start asking questions about what happens on the next page before turning it.

Remove the Sticky Tape

Although this game sounds incredibly tedious, it's

quite challenging for little people. It requires attention, fine motor skills, and problem-solving skills. If you have a couple of different colours, it's even better because it becomes more of a puzzle. Stick different lengths of tape on a surface like your fridge (something easy to clean). You can overlap a couple so that they have to peel the top colour off before the bottom.

I-Spy Adjectives

You may have already started with I-Spy Colours and it's still unlikely that they will be ready to identify letters and words. I-Spy Adjectives gives you the chance to practise vocabulary that they already know and to learn new adjectives. Try things like 'I spy something hot', 'I spy something soft', or 'I spy something small/tiny'.

Making Household Chores a Game

Do not feel guilty about getting little people involved with the cleaning. Being able to take part in simple household chores teaches them responsibility, which develops into decision-making skills and the trust in them making the right choices. And when they are older, it will also help them to respect all that parents do. At three, children should be able to put their toys away, dust the furniture, put their clothes in the laundry basket, pick up blankets and cushions from the floor, hang their coat and put their shoes away, and help lay the table.

It's all about being a game at this stage, so count toys and see if they can break their own record. Take turns in putting things on the table, and sing songs while wiping down the sides.

Make a Clean-up Tunnel

If it's hard to encourage little ones to put away their toys, you may have tried things like 'No cartoons until you finish', only for them to assume they are smarter than that and tell you they don't want to watch cartoons! Take a long cardboard tube, like the ones you find on the inside of wrapping paper. Rather than just putting toys in the basket, have them feed their toys down the tube. You can expand on this by giving them instructions like 'Put the red crayon down the tube then the blue crayon', or 'What should we put down the tube first?'.

Put the Shopping Away

Much like cleaning, putting the shopping away is not exactly exciting for adults, but these tasks are a novelty for children. They get to listen to instructions as you tell them which food to take out of the shopping bag and where to put it away. They also get to practise food vocabulary. It can help with spatial awareness and organizational skills when putting the food away.

There is a great sense of pride in knowing that they are helping Mum or Dad and getting it right, which will help their confidence. If you are the type of person who likes things to be in the exact spot, wait until they go to bed before you start adjusting the tins in the cupboard.

Hunt the Toys in Sand

Shaving foam is slightly easier, so at this age, you may want to up the game and use a sand tray or even soil if you can play outdoors. Hiding toys in the sand or soil stimulates senses like touch and even smell. If there are enough characters, pretend play can boost language and communication between you. If you are hunting the toys, you can use different tools like spades, spoons, and cups, and be sure to encourage your child to share the tools.

Stone Faces

I love this game because there are multiple aspects and benefits. The first is that you can go on a stone hunt. Describe the types of stones you need your child to find. You will need smaller round stones for the eyes, longer ones for the nose, and flatter, longer stones for the lips.

Together, you can paint parts of the face on the stones. Pro tip here, have some that you have already painted as some examples, just in case your little ones' painted features aren't quite clear. Acrylic paints work best. Be sure to have smiles, frowns, eyes with a tear, etc.

Take a piece of paper or two and draw a large, oval head shape. With the stones, make faces with different emotions, then talk about why each face might be happy, sad, angry, and so on.

How Many Socks Can You Put On?

This is a fun game that helps children to start gaining independence when getting dressed. If you struggle to keep socks on your toddler's feet, this is a good way to motivate them. Have different pairs of socks: a couple of theirs, some older siblings, and yours. Start with the smaller socks; you can help them or put them on for them. It will be easier for them to put the bigger socks on themselves. Count together the socks that they can put on.

I know I always say that you should dedicate time to play with your children but if you have to do a bit of work on the computer, donate your feet to be models for your children. They are close by and entertained while you get a couple of jobs done – and you will have lovely warm feet. Take it to the next level and give them some moisturizer for a foot massage before they put socks on your feet. Make a big deal out of their kindness!

Screen Time

We all know that screen time should be limited but in today's world, it's not practical to completely eliminate it. Nevertheless, there is a way that we can turn screen time into quality time together while boosting early interaction skills.

First of all, when it comes to the TV, try to talk together about what is on TV. What colours are there? What are the characters doing? If there is counting or an alphabet, count along or say the letters. Aim for cartoons that are specifically designed for social and emotional skills. For example, *Paw Patrol* focuses on teamwork, a sense of community, and self-confidence.

Children are naturally interested in what we are doing on our mobiles and tablets and again, it's not necessarily a bad thing that they start getting used to technology. Try to choose apps that are not only suitable for their age but will also develop skills that your child needs help with. For example, *Toca Doctor* is good for developing role-play skills because children can practise empathy by taking care of patients. *Monkey Preschool Lunchbox* is an app that toddlers won't need much parent help with.

Paint a Picture for a Friend

The idea is simple but is incredibly effective when it comes to strengthening friendships. You can talk about how their friends were feeling that day and if there was a friend who was sad, you can ask your child if they would like to make a picture for them to feel happier. Talk about the picture and ask why they think their friend would like it. Keep reminding them that the picture is for their friend so they don't think it's another one for the fridge. If, and only if, your child is comfortable, you can encourage them to give their friend a hug along with their picture.

Natural and Related Consequences Matching

Natural consequences are an amazing teaching tool that parents should learn to rely on more often because this is the foundation of cause and effect. A natural consequence would be a child refusing to wear a coat and then getting cold outside. Needless to say, this is a natural consequence for older children who theoretically know better.

For young children, a natural consequence could be hitting their friend and their friend being upset with them. A related consequence is an action you decide on to encourage or even discourage certain behaviour. For example, playing on an app after they put toys away or cleaning up a drink because they were being careless.

To make a matching game, have various cards with actions and another set with the consequences. It's a good idea to find your own pictures and make sets because then, you can focus on specific actions and consequences that will help your little one.

Happy/Sad Noughts and Crosses/Tic Tac Toe

For those who aren't sure what Noughts and Crosses is, or they can't remember, it is a grid with nine squares. The first person places a nought in a square, the next person a cross. The winner is the first person to get three noughts or crosses in a row. I like the idea of happy or sad faces, or you could also choose two different colours.

Don't worry if it takes a while for your little one to grasp the rules of this game. Be patient and gently persistent when it comes to explaining the game again. It is great for them to listen to these instructions. Plus it gives them a chance to take turns and concentrate on the problem at hand.

Chapter 7: How Is It Possible That Your Little One Is Nearly 4? What's Next?

Look through the checklist and make notes to see what your child can already do.

Early Interaction Skill	Needs More Work	In Progress	Got It
Has an extensive vocabulary of over 500 words			
Asks questions, particularly 'why' questions			
Is gaining an interest in how things work, with things like mechanical toys			
Pretend-plays with real-life situations			

such as cooking, fire rescue, etc.			
Initiates play with others			
Understands the importance of sharing and the ability to share			
Appreciates routine but is not too rigid about it			
Follows simple rules in a game			
Is becoming more independent			
Appreciates the need to tidy one set of toys before choosing another			

In many ways, life will go on much as it did in the last six months. You may find that you are settling into a new routine if your child has started nursery. If there were any signs of regression, they have probably bounced back. That being said, don't worry if this occurs now. Many parents I have spoken to have noticed sleep regression around three and a half.

You may be having some more detailed conversations and are pleasantly surprised about their ever-growing vocabulary. Other people who aren't part of the family unit will be able to understand them as pronunciation becomes clearer. On the other hand, their emotions might be getting stronger and so are the tantrums. You may have spotted them feeling more scared about imaginary things.

You might be tired and find it hard to cope with some of the emotions that are expressed around this age but it is essential for them to feel that it is okay to express their feelings instead of bottling them up. Keep reading books about emotions and feelings and ask questions about how they feel about different things.

In this chapter, we are going to look at a couple of really cool ways to help little people show you how they are feeling and to encourage other family members to do the same. But let's start with those speech sounds.

Perfect Books for Targeted Speech Sounds

Between three and a half and four, little people start working on pronouncing the /k/, /g/, /y/, /f/, /s/, and /h/ sounds. Here are just some ideas of the books that will help your little one listen and learn these sounds:

- *Duck in the Truck*
- *Big Pig on a Dig*
- *Good Morning Chick*
- *The Three Little Pigs*
- *A Fly Went By*
- *Whose Hat?*
- *Four Fur Feet*
- *Henny Penny*
- *Snowmen at Night*
- *Two Cool Cows*
- *Have You Ever Met a Yeti?*

It's Your Turn

We have looked at several games and activities that involve taking turns from cooking to I-Spy. At some point, we need to let our little ones start making decisions, and now it's their turn.

Many parents have mixed feelings about letting tiny humans make decisions. In fact, parents are often inclined only to ask questions that lead to their desired answer. As with any skill, the more it is practised, the better you become. Giving young children the chance to make some decisions teaches them about control and that their actions lead to different outcomes. Sometimes, these outcomes work in their favour, and other times not.

Making mistakes can seriously knock a person's confidence at any age. Even at this age, you can teach children that mistakes are normal, and rather than looking at them as a bad thing, you can help children learn from them.

Let's say you give your child the chance to choose dinner and they want roast chicken. They probably don't appreciate that a roast chicken takes over an hour whereas a pasta dish can be knocked up in 20 minutes. After explaining this, your child still wants roast chicken. They will have to wait. They will be hungry, but they get their delicious chicken.

The next time they get the chance to choose dinner, you can remind them of this and see if they would like to choose something a little quicker. This isn't an 'I told you so' lesson. Just opportunities for you and your child to work on making the best decisions.

A word of advice: give children the chance to make decisions when you aren't in a rush. Asking them what shoes they want to wear two minutes before walking out the door is going to stress you out!

The Emotions Thermometer

This is one of my favourites for the family to all express how they are feeling in a positive way. Draw a large thermometer on a sheet of A3 card if possible. Instead of numbers, add emotions. If you can, laminate it too because it will last longer. Have a passport photo of each family member.

Put the thermometer on the wall in a common area. The kitchen is a good idea. Just before serving dinner (as an example), have everyone put their photo on the thermometer in the place that matches their emotions. I like doing this before dinner because it is a great way to spark conversations. Ask each other why they are feeling that way and talk about what happened to cause those feelings and look at ways to solve possible problems.

Feelings Charades

You can start by making your own little charades cards either by printing emojis or drawing faces. Everybody takes a turn to pick a card and act out the emotion. If you want to expand on this game, you can add loads of different social interactions images. For example, hugs, eye contact, shaking hands, covering their mouth, saying 'Please' and 'Thank you', and so on.

Draw Your Favourite Song

This is another way for little people to express how they are feeling. Play therapists use drawing as a way for children to safely express their feelings in ways that words can't. Different songs have different meanings for different people. Let your child choose a song and play it a couple of times while they draw what it means to them.

Recycle!

I know some countries have no system and others like the UK are somewhat complex. Nevertheless, recycling provides an opportunity for children to learn about different materials and organise these materials into groups. You might want to just start with plastic, cardboard, and bottles. Even this will help them to learn about the importance of taking care of the planet, as well as having responsibilities to take care of in the home.

Don't forget about old clothes and how they can be recycled by donating to those in need. This develops empathy, while recycling our household waste develops empathy for the environment. Once they start appreciating that things can be reused, they can become more creative with their toys and materials.

Make Your Own Paintbrushes

Following on from recycling, making your own paintbrushes teaches children how to be resourceful with everyday objects instead of simply buying them. To make your own paintbrushes, collect some old twigs for the handle. You can use grass, pine needles, and some leaves to make excellent bristles.

If you want to be even more resourceful, you can make your own paint by mixing half a cup of flour, half a cup of salt, and half a cup of water. Separate the mixture and add food colouring to each one. That is literally making your own art!

Paint Me

Now that you have made all of your own materials, here is an idea for putting them to good use. Take a photo of your child and stick it onto a piece of paper. Their job is to now paint the rest of the body. If you have only made three colours, don't worry. I always say go for blue, red, and yellow because these primary colours will allow you to mix others. When children mix colours, they are learning to observe. You can ask them to predict what colour will be made and of course, there is cause and effect – all valuable science skills.

Number Stacking

Your little one might be getting the hang of the numbers from 1 to 10. They may have also started counting up to 20 although it's perfectly normal that some numbers are skipped. Choose a simple object like a car or a flower, draw a few, and cut them out. In the middle, write a number – they don't have to be in order. The idea is that your child stacks the correct number of blocks, bricks, Lego, etc., that corresponds to the number on the image. Apart from practising counting, they are also learning how to recognise written numbers.

We're Going on a Nature Hunt

I always try to get at least one outdoor activity in each chapter. This is because getting out and about in nature has been shown to greatly reduce stress in adults, as well as in children. It makes a nice change to put those scenes away and get some gentle exercise with a walk.

Why not pique the interests of your little one by setting them a challenge while out on a walk? Take some of the paint you made and paint patches on a piece of card, closer to the edges. In the middle, you can add a nice title. For each colour, add a peg – if you have some of the smaller craft pegs they might be better. While you are on your walk, get them to find something that matches each colour you have painted.

A nature hunt boosts curiosity and investigative skills. There is also a massive amount of pride when all of their pegs are full.

Rice Rainbows

If you want to use pasta you can, but you may find that this will be too easy for them and you do want to make some of your activities a little challenging. Separate some rice into a few bowls and add different food colourings to each. How many bowls and how much rice will depend on how many colours you want in the rainbow and how big your picture will be. Be brave and ask your child to make the decision!

It's a good idea to leave the rice to dry a little so it doesn't end up dying their fingers. Put some PVC glue in an arch shape on the paper and ask them to spoon some rice to make the first colour of the rainbow. To make it easier, you can draw a rainbow so they just need to fill between the lines with the rice. You could also do the first arch for them. To make it harder, ask them to spread the glue before the rice.

This will require your child to first listen to your instructions. It will also take a surprising amount of attention and concentration to get the rice into rainbow arches and hopefully without too much rice mixing into other colours.

Make Yourself Like a...

Those little meltdowns caused by boredom can easily be resolved by a quick game of Make Yourself Like a... If you are waiting in line at the supermarket or the waiting room at the doctors, take advantage to practise those adjectives and nouns. Here are some examples:

- Make yourself like a tall tree
- Make yourself like a tiny rock
- Make yourself like a scary bear
- Make yourself like a metal robot
- Make yourself like a cute puppy

Dot to Dots

Naturally, you should start with simple dot to dots and it might help to use the dots that have arrows to help them see what direction they should join the dots in. You don't even need to print images because you can make simple dot to dots yourself.

Dot to dots are going to give your child time to practise gripping a pencil, which is going to help them with their handwriting. Social skills include communication, and communication is defined as verbal and non-verbal – writing! They also have the opportunity to improve hand-eye coordination and their understanding of the link between cause and effect.

Face Painting

Again, it's fine to go and buy a set of face paints but if you want to extend the activity, you can make your own. If you make your own, your child is also working together with you and listening to your instructions. Here is a recipe for homemade face paints:

- 1 cup water
- 1 cup corn starch
- 1 cup flour
- 1 cup moisturiser
- ¼ tsp vegetable oil

Start by mixing the water, corn starch, flour, and lotion in a bowl. Then add the other ingredients. More corn starch will thicken the paint and more water will thin it out. Separate the mixture into different containers and add your food colourings.

Face painting is great fun for little ones and it lets them use their imagination. It is also a very good activity to help them improve eye contact as you will be face-to-face.

Toilet Roll People

By now, you may have noticed just how handy the inside of a toilet roll is. There are tons of animal patterns you can use online, even Father Christmas and other Christmas characters if you are looking for holiday-specific decorations. I like toilet roll people because you can use them for emotions and pretend play.

If you have some pipe cleaners, these make great arms and legs. You can draw the faces on. If you have any rags or clothes, you can make clothes if you want to. Again, if you want to, you can use wool or cotton wool.

Chapter 8: Your 4-Year-Old Thinks They Know Best – But You Can Still Help Them to Be Better

Look through the checklist and make notes to see what your child can already do.

Early Interaction Skill	Needs More Work	In Progress	Got It
Is beginning to understand morals, fairness, and recognise correct behaviour			
Is becoming more aware of other people's emotions			
Listens to others and respects turn-taking in conversations			
Is showing more concentration on			

tasks for a longer period of time			
Recognises all of the letters of the alphabet and begins to copy some			
Understands that they have some simple responsibilities and sticks to them			
Shows good manners with 'please', 'thank you', and 'excuse me'			
Accepts diversity and differences between people			
Has a toy or activity that calms them down			

Has a strong group of friends and probably a best friend			

I'm always looking at different people's opinions, advice, and research with the aim of providing the most varied information for every parent and child. This latest that I came across sparked a bit of interest and I would be keen to know your thoughts.

This goes back to the idea of an activity that keeps children engaged for the most amount of time possible. Not because we are lazy parents, but because we are busy, we don't want children to sit in front of the TV, and we know that boredom often leads to meltdowns.

For this, we look for toys that are, for a better word, multi-purpose. They have voices, actions, lights, and so on. Naturally, if you are going to invest in a toy, you want it to last more than five minutes.

The most amazing tip I recently learnt that will help children between the age of four and four and a half [JM3]is that the less a toy does, the more a child learns. And trust me, when you understand the logic behind this, it makes so much sense for various age groups.

Think back to a favourite toy you had when you were younger. I remember I had a doll called Robin. He had a blue sleepsuit and nothing else! There couldn't have been a toy that did less. Compare that to one of today's dolls that eats, drinks, cries, has a nap, needs a bath, and so on. Playtime is dominated by the doll and not the imagination. With dear little Robin, I had to make up the stories, find materials for a bed, and make Play-Doh food. And so the theory 'the less a toy does, the more a child learns' makes perfect sense. Try to remember this as your child is encouraged by toys with all the bells and whistles. Of course, it's normal to want toys that are full of action but it's good to have a balance.

In this chapter, I will list some new games and play ideas but I will also cover a few that you may have used for previous stages and discuss how you can adapt them.

Perfect Books for Targeted Speech Sounds

Once a child hits four, there is often some development with blended sounds, particularly with the /l/ and /r/. For example, /bl/, /vl/, /fl/, /gl/, /br/, /cr/, /dr/, /fr/, /gr/, /pr/, and /tr/ at the beginning of words. At the end of words, they will start using /ks/, /ls/, /ms/, /ps/, /ts/, and /vs/. These are quite a few new sounds so here are some ideal books to work on these blended sounds.

- *Cows Can't Fly*
- *I Love Planes*
- *Slip! Slide! Skate!*
- *Flip-Flops*
- *Sledding*
- *Big Frank's Fire Truck*
- *A Crack in the Track*
- *Five Green Speckled Frogs*
- *Little Green Truck*
- *Froggy Gets Dressed*

The Obstacle Course

Now that they are a lot more stable and have increased their range of motion, it's time to go back to the obstacle course and make it more challenging. Add some activities that include squeezing through gaps or even a mental challenge in the middle like a simple crossword. The idea isn't just to make the obstacle course harder, but they should also have to pay greater attention to the instructions.

Counting Pasta

By four, children are often confident with counting to 20 but that's not to say that this won't need some reinforcement. Of course, if you give a four-year-old some pasta and ask them to count, it you can probably expect your first 'lame parent' look.

Instead, set different counting challenges, maybe even while they are painting the pasta or threading it onto string to make necklaces because this will help those fine motor skills too. Start with 10 pieces of pasta and count backward. Or count together in twos. They might take a while to learn these new concepts but it's an excellent start while building focus.

The Fill the Post Box Game

We saw how to turn a simple cardboard box into a post box. Hopefully, your little one recycled that box so it might be time to get a new one and maybe even decorate it up as a character they like instead of a post box. Use the mouth as the slot.

Last time, we used emotions. This time, draw letters and hide some of them around the room. Although you can draw all the letters now, hiding all 26 will be too much because their attention is unlikely to hold. Maybe start with hiding five letters that they recognise. If they enjoy the first five and want to continue playing, you can either add a few more letters or change the set.

The Staring Game

It goes without saying that the staring game is going to help those all-important eye contact skills that are required when having conversations. If you have noticed that your child appears uncomfortable when making eye contact, don't challenge them to stare at you because they will only feel worse. Start by placing stickers on your foreheads and see how long you can stare at the sticker.

Once they get the hang of this, don't be scared to shake it up a little. Generally speaking, we try to focus on one activity so that children aren't distracted. Nevertheless, in the real world, we often have to make eye contact as we are doing other things like talking, folding the washing, even playing. Add some conversation to your game and if you're feeling really keen, you can try stacking Lego bricks as you stare.

Watch Bluey!

We have already mentioned that it's very hard to completely prevent children from watching TV. But we can make sure they are watching games that inspire social interactions. And you can't go wrong with a cartoon that makes both kids and parents giggle.

Bluey is all about a little dog, her sister Bingo, and Mum and Dad. Each episode is about different games the family invent together using everyday objects from around the house, or entertaining themselves when they are out and about. There are some great, valuable lessons like not always getting what you want and how to get your parents' attention the right way.

This little Australian family of dogs can be found on YouTube, if it's not on your TV channels.

My First Map

I always feel that this is the type of activity that suits a rainy day where nobody wants to go out. That being said, if you have a garden, it's just as good to do outside. With a piece of paper, mark the outline of the area you want to map. Make sure your child sees how you look around the area as you draw each bit. They need to learn that this activity requires observation. The skill level and how much you get involved will determine the area to map. It might be just one room or you can draw one floor.

Have your child look around the room and add different pieces of furniture. Another idea is to cut furniture out of newspapers and magazines and have them stick the furniture in the corresponding locations. Your child's first map will help with spatial reasoning and a look into geography. It may not seem specifically like an interaction skill, but you do still need to provide activities that will make them feel confident in the classroom.

Community Gardening

Planting seeds is a wonderful responsibility for children because they have something to take care of and are learning about nature. When you combine this with community gardening, you have some important social skills that are developed when interacting with others. Even though I'm speaking as the type of person who can kill a cactus, I will still say that gardening with others is a way to learn about different types of plants and even fruit and vegetables you can grow.

If there are no community gardening groups in your area, you can easily create one with a few friends and family members – even better if they have children too. You can use each other's gardens or if you are feeling super-motivated about this idea, speak to your local council to see if there is a small plot of land that could be used to create a community garden. With the current climate crisis, it should be hard for them to say no!

Create a Mini-Me

Drawings are great, but at this age, creating life-sized mini-mes is so much more fun. There are two ways you can do this. The first is to have them lie down on paper (look for rolls of tablecloth paper because this is always handy). Once the outline is done, they can draw their own features – have them look in a mirror to copy their eyes and nose.

Now, if you are the sort of person who collects boxes to reuse, you could see if you have enough different shapes and sizes to create a mini-me out of boxes. For arms and legs, poke a hole in the ends of kitchen roll holders and join them together with string – now you have elbows and knees. Gloves can be attached for hands, a balloon for the head, and a mop for hair.

Use your mini-me for role play and pretend play!

Revise the Chores Chart

Chore charts by age are a great way to remind parents exactly what their children are capable of doing around the house. Children who take part in household chores are going to be more responsible, and this will reflect in school when it comes to taking care of their pencil case, books, and doing homework. There is a direct influence of social skills on the independence of young children (Journal of Educational Science and Technology, 2019).

At four, children will be able to (or at least start to) feed pets, wipe up spilt drink, water plants, use a lightweight vacuum cleaner, help clear the table, put away clean cutlery, and start keeping their bedrooms tidier. If you have started with chores early, it will be easier to motivate children to do these jobs. If not, don't forget to make a game out of it, like musical vacuuming, where they have to stand still when the music stops.

Family Contest

I say 'Family' but this can also be with friends and it doesn't have to be the same age. The idea of the game is to think of different challenges that cover a wide range of abilities and aren't related to intelligence. Some examples might include:

- Who can touch their nose with their tongue?
- Who can jump the highest?
- Who can stand on one leg for the longest?
- Who can make a paper aeroplane the fastest... and whose flies the farthest?
- Who can stack the most bricks?

This game is invaluable for teaching diversity. It shows children that we are all different and some of us are better at some things than others. While we can all work on our skills, we don't have to be the best at everything.

Finish the Story

By now, your child will have a good understanding of different stories and how they end. If your child picks up their favourite book, read the first few pages and ask them what happens next. Then propose a question where they have to think of an alternative ending. Here is an example:

'A mouse took a stroll through the deep dark woods... first he met a fox, then the owl.' Ask your child what animal they meet next. They are expecting the snake. Ask your child 'What if instead of a snake, the mouse meets rabbit?'.

This activity will help children to resolve problems on the spot instead of knowing the outcome beforehand. If you are using social stories, this will help children explore the different outcomes of everyday situations that they may otherwise struggle with.

Virtual Playdates

Socialising today is certainly not the same as it was just a couple of years ago. Whether you have restrictions in place or not, it may not be so simple to just set up a playdate and have others come to your house. But just as businesses have turned to virtual communications, there is no reason why you can't do the same.

Virtual playdates or even video chats with family members teaches children how to use crucial social skills in a different way. There is a whole online etiquette for eye contact and turn-taking – you know what it's like when either everyone is talking or nobody is talking. Learning how to adapt social skills to the virtual world will be a crucial skill for children in the future.

Lego Therapy

If you haven't started Lego Therapy yet, this type of play is excellent at this age because the children are able to play each role independently. For those who need a little practice in patience, you can use Lego Therapy to remind them that giving people instructions requires a calm voice, and that sometimes we need to explain things in different ways for others to understand.

A quick recap on Lego Therapy. There are three roles, the Architect, the Supplier, and the Builder. With an object to build, the Architect has to give instructions to the Supplier on the materials needed and how to build it, while the Builder makes it. They can take turns to play each role.

Alphabet Maze

All you need is some paper and a toy car or toy animal. Cut pieces of paper up into strips and line them on the floor to make a maze. Then write the letters of the alphabet on pieces of paper (or use the letters from the post box game). Line the maze with the letters.

With the toy car or animal, ask the children to follow the letters in the correct order. It's a different way for children to practise the alphabet but they are also practising some problem-solving skills – and agility, if they are to move around the maze without moving the paper.

FREE Goodwill

He who said money can't buy happiness hasn't given enough away. By Anonymous

People who help others with zero expectations experience higher level of fulfillment, live longer and make more money.

I want to create an opportunity to deliver this value to you during your reading or listening experience. In order to do so I have one simple ask, would you help someone you have never met, it wouldn't cost you any money and you'll never get credit for it?

If so then I have a request on behalf of someone you do not know and likely never will meet.

They are just like you or like you were a few months/years ago, less experienced and full of desire to help their child, seeking information but unsure where to look. This is where you come in.

The only way for us at **Kids SLT Publishing** to accomplish our mission of helping parents this first by reaching them, and most people do in fact judge a book by its cover and its reviews.

If you have found this book valuable and helpful thus far, would you please take a moment right now and leave an honest review of the book and its contents. It will cost you zero pounds/dollars and takes less than 60 seconds.

Your review will help those parents who are looking for advice and strategies to help their child.

- Your review will help another child reach their potential
- your review will help another parent feel better that they have found a helpful resource
- your review will help a parent feel less anxious and more confident in their abilities with the help of this book.
- Your review will help one more life change for the better

To do this, all you have to do is, and it only takes less than 60 seconds, is to leave a review. If you are on audible click the three dots and choose 'review'.

If you are on Kindle, click the link below which will take you to the Amazon book page, scroll down the page and leave a review.

http://mybook.to/SLT4Toddlers

If you are reading a paperback please search for this book on Amazon, click on the book, scroll down the page, and click on 'leave customer review'. If you don't have time to write a review, you can leave star rating only but even a sentence would be extremely valuable.

If you introduce something valuable to someone, they will associate that value with you. If you would like goodwill directed from another parent then send this book their way

Thank you from the bottom of our heart, and now back to your regular programming!

http://mybook.to/SLT4Toddlers

Chapter 9: From 4½–5 – The Last Boost Before School

Look through the checklist and make notes to see what your child can already do.

Early Interaction Skill	Needs More Work	In Progress	Got It
Has a greater understanding of cooperation			
Enjoys playing mum and dad			
Has a keen interest to explore new places and things			
Has an understanding of what's real and what's pretend			

Shows self-regulation – they understand how they are feeling and is getting better at controlling it			
Writes their name and draws more realistic pictures			
Recognises around 20 sight words			
Is starting to want to please friends and parents			
Performs pretend play that is becoming more structured and organized			
Understands and agrees to the rules of games and activities			

Much like nursery, different countries and even areas can start school at slightly different ages, but between four and a half and five, most children will be getting those sparkling new school supplies ready in their shiny backpacks.

Supplies are only the half of it. Make sure you are taking advantage of these months to fully prepare them for all the new social interactions. There are a lot of new sounds between four and five years old. Let's start by helping develop some of the sounds from the last chapter, as well as books that will target new sounds.

Practising Those Blended Sounds

I came across a great set of worksheets that you can print or make your own versions of. I particularly like the 'R Blends' sheet, where you can cut the different /r/ blends and children can stick them onto the page next to the correct picture.

Because their vocabulary will be quite extensive now, you can also play the 'Name Three More' game. Say and/or write a word with one of the blended sounds. For a recap, these are /bl/, /cl/, /fl/, /gl/, /br/, /cr/, /dr/, /fr/, /gr/, /pr/, /tr/, and for the endings of words, /ks/, /ls/, /ms/, /ps/, /ts/, and /vs/.

For example, you write and say 'Clever'. Then, they have to think of three more words that begin with the same sound.

Perfect Books for Targeted Speech Sounds

You will also find that many books now will have plenty of blended sounds that will help develop the previous sounds. The list below is going to help with the /v/, /z/, /sh/, /ch/, /j/, and /l/ sounds.

- *Itchy, Itchy Chicken Pox*
- *The Giant Jam Sandwich*
- *If I Ran the Zoo*
- *Zip, Whiz, Zoom!*
- *Does a Kangaroo Have a Mother Too?*
- *I Love You, Stinky Face*
- *Smile Lily*
- *Sheep in a Shop*
- *Whose Nose?*
- *Leo the Late Bloomer*
- *Making Plum Jam*

The Emotion Thermometer

Let's revamp the old emotion thermometer, or it's probably better to start a fresh one, and update those photos too. With the start of school, there is going to be a rush of new emotions, and you should try to help your little ones express these feelings as accurately as possible.

Here are some typical feelings children have when starting school:

- Sad
- Worried
- Lonely
- Overwhelmed
- Proud
- Excited
- Confused
- Surprised

Of course, you might need to explain the meaning of some of these emotions. Put them into context with an experience that has caused them to feel this particular emotion. Also, try to make sure there is a balance of positive and negative emotions.

At a sensible time – dinner is best – everyone can put their photo on the thermometer according to their feelings. If you want to have two photos, children can choose two different emotions and understand that it's perfectly normal to have mixed emotions.

The Marshmallow Test

This is an excellent 'test' that really is like a game for little people. It was originally used with a marshmallow but you can use any type of treat – although it does have to be enticing. Put the treat on a plate and tell them that they can have the treat now, or they can wait 10 minutes and have double.

This 1972 test was created by Professor Walter Mischel at Stanford University. He used it to measure how well children were able to delay gratification in order to receive a bigger reward later on.

The results of his test showed that children who were able to wait did better academically. As teenagers, they handled stress better and as adults, they had healthier relationships as adults.

The Marshmallow Test is a great way to teach patience and perseverance. These skills are going to be excellent not only for school, but also for social interactions outside of the classroom.

Guess Who

The classic game of Guess Who involves two sets of characters, and two headbands. A character is placed in the headband and the person wearing the headband has to guess who it is. If you don't want to buy the game, you can print off Guess Who bingo-like worksheets.

There are many benefits to Guess Who. Children are practising asking questions and they have to pay close attention to the answers and remember them. I also like Guess Who because it's another way to teach about diversity. If you are playing with characters on the forehead, it's also good for eye contact.

The Fill the Post Box Game

This game is an update of the game from two previous chapters because it is such a good one. Take a simple box, create an opening, and decorate the box. Before, you were using emotions and then letters.

Now, you can start playing the same game but using words. At first, you can start with common sight words, such as the pronouns, 'wh' question words, and some verbs like 'have', 'come', 'do', and 'go'. To increase the difficulty, you can hide words, give the child a sentence, and ask them to post the words in the order of a sentence. You can also start to hide the words in more challenging places.

I Hear With My Little Ear

It's rare that a child will get bored with I Spy, but this handy adaptation is amazing for getting them to really focus on the sounds around them. When you are choosing sounds, you will have to make sure they are sounds that can be heard for long enough for them to guess.

Apart from listening skills, this game will help children to identify objects based on their sounds, rather than what they look like. If you can't find any suitable sounds, you can use the Internet to find various sounds.

Follow the Grid Game

If you want to help your child improve their listening skills while following directions and learning about spatial awareness, the grid game ticks all the boxes. You can also work on left and right and even move in diagonal directions.

Take some string or strips of cardboard and lay them out on the floor to make a grid. Each square needs to be big enough for children to comfortably fit their foot inside. A good size would be around 6 x 6 inches.

Have your child stand in one square and give them directions like 'Move one square to the left', or 'Move two squares forward'. You can start with one direction at a time but then you could start giving two or three directions.

If you want to add some patience, put some of their favourite toys in some of the squares. As much as they will want to move to the square with their toy, they have to wait for your directions.

What Should Mummy/Daddy Do?

Children need to learn how to listen to instructions, but they also need to learn how to give them in a kind and respectful way. To help with this, you can ask your child to tell you how to do certain tasks. Really, you have to think about tasks that they know how to do or they have at least seen you do plenty of times.

One example could be cooking. If you have made cupcakes (or another simple recipe) together various times, you can ask them to walk you through all of the steps. So, they would start by telling you what equipment and ingredients you need. Then how to measure the ingredients, and so on.

You can also use other tasks like making the shopping list. Here, your child would tell you which cupboards, shelves, fridge/freezer to check for food that is needed.

This activity might actually be harder for you than it is for them, in some ways. A lot of our daily tasks are automatic. We don't need to think about the steps. If our child tells us the wrong step, our mind and body will keep going with how we normally would do it.

Rather than tell them that they made a mistake, ask if they can repeat what they said. This is often enough for them to rethink and correct their own mistakes. If it's something that won't have huge consequences, you can follow their instructions and see what happens.

If they get frustrated because they can't remember or they can't explain a step, help them to calm down and talk about the next step together. Offer different suggestions and encourage them to choose the right one. Give them lots of praise so they are motivated to finish all of the instructions.

It's Your Turn

Social interactions rely heavily on the interests of your child. You know full well that your levels of social interactions change, depending on the activity you are doing. A school meeting isn't the same as catching up with friends.

Every once in a while, let your child choose. This could be the family entertainment, meal, the games they want to play, or even the conversation topic. Children's interests change very quickly, and letting them have a turn allows you insights into these new interests. It also teaches them that their opinions matter. When it comes to their own social interactions, they will lead by this example and give their friends a turn.

Developing 'Wh' Questions

Awkward silences are just something we adults have to deal with. When children struggle to maintain a conversation, they can become nervous and introverted. This can follow them around and cause them to be shy in other social situations. You can encourage them to make questions in everyday situations, but you can also make a game out of it.

Take one of their toys and tell your child that they need to investigate who they are and what they are doing. Prepare ahead and have the background prepared in your mind. Let's look at an example.

'I have a dinosaur in my hand. He is going to a party with his dinosaur friends. He is excited because there will be music and cake – he loves cake. He is a little nervous because there will be new friends. He has a toothbrush as a present so his dinosaur friend can keep his teeth nice and clean.'

Your child can ask questions like:

- What is its name?
- How old is it?
- What is it doing?
- Where is it going?
- What is it taking?
- How does the dinosaur feel?

The more questions they can ask, the more creative your answers may get, and this will lead to more questions.

Sensory Alphabet Hunt

It can be as messy as you want to make it! There are so many materials you can use, from shaving foam, sand, and soil to rice or small pebbles. You can even mix two different materials together. Take a small set of alphabet letters and hide them in the tray.

When your child finds a letter, they can put it to one side. But try to encourage them to put the letters in order as they find each one.

Lily Pad Sight Words

If you have already made sight words for the post box game, you can recycle them for this game. The idea is to make different lily pads and stick them to the floor. It's better to use something stronger than paper because as children jump from one to the other, the paper can rip. Also, be sure to have a good range of words so that you can create different sentences.

Place your lily pads on the floor and give your child a sentence. Have them stand on the lily pad with the first word of the sentence. From there, they have to jump from one pad to another to complete the sentence you said.

Puffy Paint

If you are looking for a way to promote creativity with paints but in a very different way, you can use puffy paint. As with other painting activities, this will help with self-expression, hand-eye coordination, and fine motor development. There is also an amazing sense of pride for children when they get to try something new.

Of course, you might have noticed by now that I am a bit of a fan of homemade whenever possible. Here is how you make your own puffy paint.

Mix one tablespoon of self-raising flour with a tablespoon of salt. Then add 3 teaspoons of water and mix well. Add a few drops of food colouring. You can repeat the same steps for each colour, or make one large batch and separate it before adding the food colouring.

Once your little one has created their masterpiece, place it in the microwave on top of a microwave-proof bowl. Every microwave is different but it takes around 20–25 seconds for the paint to puff.

Bottle Top Money

While it's true most of us hardly ever have cash on us now, we still need to teach children about the value of money. As pretend play gets more detailed, toy money can be used to play in shops, hairdressers, or petrol stations, and so on.

Collect different-sized bottle caps. Print multiple images of coins and stick them to the bottle tops. Make sure that each coin value has the same size bottle top. So all of your 50p coins will be milk bottle lids, all £1 coins will be cola bottle lids, etc.

To extend the game, you can start explaining how two 10p pieces are the same value as one 20p coin. And how certain objects cost more than others. These are difficult concepts for little people, but there is no harm in starting if they are keen to play.

Chapter 10: Bonus Play Ideas for the Over 5s to Feel More Confident with Friends, Family, and Teachers

Look through the checklist and make notes to see what your child can already do.

Early Interaction Skill	Needs More Work	In Progress	Got It
Is starting to develop a sense of self-esteem			
Understands their mistakes and learns from them			
Is beginning to listen to other people's opinions			
Is more sensitive and empathetic towards others' feelings			

Can make choices between more than two options			
Sees that there are consequences to their actions			
Expresses their needs in the right way, without getting frustrated or angry			
Shows compassion for people in difficult social situations, such as poverty			
Wants to help others			
Asks for help when needed			

My main area of speciality is up to the age of five but of course, that's not to say that as the clock chimes on their fifth birthday, children are all of a sudden ready for social interactions. There will be new challenges as well as some ups and downs, and it's great if parents have the knowledge, resources, and confidence to support their children in these years.

I also felt that this chapter would help any parents who have older children and are slightly worried about their social interactions. It might not be the case that they need professional support, but just a few extra games and activities with the family can be enough to make a huge improvement.

Don't forget that any of the ideas from the previous chapters where you have been using them and seeing results can still be used now. You are the best person to see how your child is progressing and how you can tweak activities to make them easier or harder. At the end of the day, you want your children to have fun and be happy, so if they have favourite activities, encourage them to keep doing them.

Let's begin this chapter in the same way, with a focus on developing speech sounds.

Perfect Books for Targeted Speech

Between the age of five and six, children will be working on /r/ and /th/. They will also be perfecting the blended sounds /sp/, /sm/, /sn/, /sk/, /sl/, /sw/, /st/, /str/, /skr/, /spl/, /the/, and /shr/. If you haven't read any of Julia Donaldson's books (*The*

Gruffalo, Room on the Broom) this is a great place to start. You can also look for *Songbird Phonics*, a series of 60 books created by Julia Donaldson with Oxford Reading Tree.

- *Piranhas Don't Eat Bananas*
- *The Very Noisy Bear*
- *Pocket Dogs and the Lost Kitten*
- *Don't Think About Purple Elephants*
- *Come Down, Cat!*
- *Big Rain Coming* (also good for learning about diversity)
- *The Girl Who Never Made Mistakes* (also good for teaching that mistakes are normal)
- *Freddie and the Fairy*
- *Wombat Stew*
- *Hands Are Not for Hitting*

How to Encourage a Love for Reading

The age that children start to pick up a book and read independently can range from four to six or even seven. Sadly, for one reason or another, not all children will naturally develop this love, and forcing them is likely to promote the opposite desire.

Comic books have never really received the credit they deserve. We often assume that they are simplified books for more action than words. This is far from the case and can make reading a lot more enjoyable for young readers who are put off by books.

There are also more visual clues that can give children more confidence.

The University of Oregon Center on Teaching and Learning found that comic books have an average of 53.5 rare words for every thousand words. Children's books have an average of 30.9 rare words per thousand. So comics can actually expand a child's vocabulary. Here are some ideas for comic books:

- *Owly* (series) – good for younger children and problem-solving skills
- *El Deafo* – based on the author's personal experience of losing her hearing when she was four
- *Hilo* (series) – funny stories about friendships
- *The Cardboard Kingdom* – cooperation, creativity, and empathy
- *Hilda* (series) – based on the *Hilda* Netflix series
- *Guts* – one of many from Raina Tegemeier, this focuses on preteen health issues that are often taboo subjects

Word Building

This activity will really help children who are struggling with reading, writing, and spelling, regardless of their age. You can buy activities like this but it's just as easy to make your own.

Start by taking a piece of card. I would laminate it so that you can write on it with a felt-tip and wipe it off afterward. Then, write various different words clearly (not in cursive) and cut the words up into their separate syllables. If your child is younger, start with simple two-syllable sight words like 'father', which you would cut into 'fa' and 'ther' or 'river', cut as 'ri' and 'ver'.

With a felt-tip, write your word on the laminated card and ask your child to find the correct syllables to make the word underneath your written word. Again, if they are younger, you can start with a smaller selection of syllables and show them how to make different words first. You can also tie this in with the key vocabulary they are learning at school.

Taking Turns in Storytelling

It's a good idea to use this as a creative activity rather than telling favourite stories from books or comics. You or your child can begin with the first sentence or two of a story. Then the next person adds their part, and so on. Older children might be able to make up half or even an entire story.

Listen carefully, because they might be telling you a story or a difficult time they went through and you have a chance to show empathy and encourage them to share their feelings.

If you are starting a story about yourself, this is a great chance to share information that they would otherwise not know. For example, you can talk about yourself as a child or hobbies that you liked then and still like. See if they can summarise the parts of your story and show empathy to any challenges you have.

If your child finds it hard to ignore distractions, take turns, or stick to time limits, you can use a timer to help them stay focused. To help them further, play this game in an area where there are fewer distractions. Practising in quieter areas will help them when it comes to busier areas like the classroom.

Sharing Is Caring

One of the best ways to set an amazing example for work ethic and sharing is to sit down together to do your 'homework'. There are tons of jobs that require us to sit down for 15 to 30 minutes – it could be paying the bills, returning a few emails, or working on the family budget. At the same time, they may have homework, or a fun worksheet that you would like them to do, or just reading.

Sit together at the table, where you have your materials and they have theirs. You can also include your snack/drink and theirs. Together, work on your tasks, sharing each other's objects when necessary. Even if you don't need their rubber, ask for it once in a while because it's a good way to show them that you sometimes make mistakes too.

If they won't share, talk about how this upsets you. When they do share or use words like 'please' and 'thank you', praise them for their good manners.

Role Play the Harder Things

The reason I suggest leaving this for the older children is that they have to understand that if you make a comment during this game, it is part of the game and not an accusation. If at any point you can sense that they aren't gaining, change the activity.

Let your child be the teaser or the bully first, and ask them to tease you. They could say 'You're stupid' and you can respond in a calm way with 'Sorry you think that' or 'I'm not interested in your opinions'.

Role-playing situations like this give children a turn to practise self-regulation and not give bullies the reaction they are hoping for. As bullying is still such a common occurrence, encourage your child to talk to someone if they are struggling with this issue.

Break out the Board Games

Board games are awesome for playing with friends and family, whether that's *Monopoly*, *The Game of Life*, or *Trouble*, or card games like *Go Fish* and *Uno*. You have a huge range of skills to practise, from listening to directions, taking turns, cooperation, and of course, they can learn how to deal with losing and the challenging feelings that may come with it.

Challenge Time

While developing social skills with the activities I have talked about here, I haven't been suggesting that you actually label them and ask your child to think about when they are using these skills. Try challenging your child with these:

- Tell me three times you took turns today
- Tell me four times when you used body language today
- Tell me the names of five people you made eye contact with
- Tell me about one situation when you had to change the way you were talking

Talking about our social interactions helps us to highlight how important they are and how frequently we use them, possibly without even noticing.

Would You Rather...

This is a simple speaking activity that encourages children to make decisions and justify their answers. So, if you ask them 'Would you rather eat frogs' legs or jump out of an aeroplane?' If they said, 'Jump out of an aeroplane', they would have to give you a reason, like 'Frogs legs must be all bony and have no meat'.

The only limit to this game is your imagination. 'Would you rather sleep in a waterbed or on a boat?' 'Would you like to eat ice cream for the rest of your life or chocolate?' It's a fun and insightful game that can also involve turn-taking and it will help children become more confident.

After School Activities

Obviously, most schools offer a good range of after-school clubs and activities, but try not to rely solely on these. One potential problem is that the school doesn't offer an activity that your child is excited about and they feel forced into the typical dance or football clubs. The other problem is that if they are having difficulties making friends in school, they might have the same challenges in after-school clubs with the same peers.

Look at sports clubs, town halls, and city councils to see the full range of activities available. This will also give children a chance to meet new people and of course make new friends. The skills they use can be transferred into the classroom and along with more confidence, this should produce some improvements with school friends.

Anger Drawing

Children, just like us adults, are going to feel angry at times and we shouldn't be telling them to block this feeling or replace it with a more positive one. There is a genuine reason why they have any emotion and the healthy way to deal with it is to label it and talk about solutions.

A good way to do this is to say something like 'I can see you are feeling angry. Why don't we make a drawing of your anger and give it a name?' This separates the child from the anger. Now, they can recognize that they aren't an angry person, but they feel anger.

With a drawing, children can now see the problem. In this manner, the distance from the emotion will help them discover ways to overcome the problem.

Video Games That Help Develop Social Skills

Video games are much like comics in that they have a bit of a bad reputation. It's true that having children glued to a screen for hours on end is not good. Nevertheless, as technology is going to be an integral part of their future, children also need to get confident with it at a young age.

Various games have different objectives. To a non-player, they might look like a load of characters trying to kill each other but games do help improve spatial skills, which in turn, helps them with STEM (science, technology, engineering and math) skills.

Games like *World of Warcraft*, *Trove*, and *Neverwinter* are massive, multiplayer online role-playing games, or MMORPGs. In these, players need to interact and coordinate with other players if they want to achieve their goals.

Write a Gratitude Letter

Writing a simple and short letter to a friend or relative gives children the chance to express their emotions, let others know why they are special, and why they are grateful for them in their lives.

You can lead by example and write a little letter to your child. Encourage a reply by ending the letter with 'Hope to hear back soon'. This will also help them to structure their own letter. If you are feeling creative, add a little drawing too.

Make an Art Frame

Whether it's a favourite photo or a drawing they have done, you can really make it special by adding a homemade nature frame. Plus, it gets you out of the house to hunt for materials. You need four sticks that are long enough for the photo or art. You can also collect some leaves or flowers to decorate the frame.

With some thread, tie all four corners together. You can also continue wrapping threads around the sticks if you want to add some colour. Attach the leaves and flowers with glue.

This activity is great for resourcefulness and taking advantage of things in nature rather than buying things. There is also plenty of creativity and listening to instructions. Finally, they will feel an even greater sense of pride.

Sofa Time

Finally, just take some time to sit on the sofa with your children. Read books, watch TV together, or talk about each other's day. We live in a world that is non-stop crazy from work to school, homework and clubs, housework, and so on. Everyone needs a little bit of downtime to rest and enjoy the moment. Don't feel guilty for this snuggling session because your children will love it more than you know... It won't be long before they are teenagers and you will miss it.

Chapter 11: How to Start Using Social Stories with Children of All Ages

Social stories and comic strip conversations were originally created by Carol Gray in 1991. The idea was to help people with autism feel safe in situations that would otherwise cause them to feel anything from uneasy to sheer panic. Today, they can be used to help anyone in a wide range of social situations.

What Are Social Stories?

A social story is a short story or description of an event that gives children an idea of what to expect. They can be used for self-care, like getting dressed, or to help with social skills such as sharing. They can be created to show the best way to handle difficult emotions or changes in routine that could cause these strong feelings.

We all know that children are huge fans of routine, and any situation that throws a routine out of balance can be hard for them to cope with. By reading social stories together, you can help them to plan and prepare for this change. Best of all, they can be adapted to meet the needs of your child.

What's the Difference Between a Social Story and a Comic Strip Conversation?

Social stories tell a tale that can describe a specific situation like going to the doctor. They can include pictures or even photos. A comic strip conversation uses stick figures that talk to each other about a situation. I will give an example of each later on.

There are plenty of social stories that you can buy or download but it is better to try and create your own so that you can personalize it. For example, if you are taking your nervous little one to the dentist, your social story might include an older sibling who will be there to go first.

How to Create Your Own Social Stories

According to Gray's 2015 book, *The New Social Story Book*, there are three steps to creating your own social stories: understand the goal, gather the information, and then tailor the text.

1. **Understand the goal:** what is it you want to achieve from the story? It might be that they are fighting with their siblings over toys. So the goal would be to emphasize sharing so that both children are happier during playtime.
2. **Gather the information:** who are the characters, and where does the story begin and end? Consider the age and interests of the child

so you can choose the appropriate language level and images.

3. **Tailor the text:** this is the introduction, the middle, and the end. It goes into descriptions of the who, what, where, when, why, and how. It also includes some coaching sentences so that children learn the appropriate behaviour.

When writing a social story, write in the first person (using "I"). For this, you have to imagine yourself as the child because they are the one who has to relate to the story.

What to Do When You Don't Feel Creative Enough to Write Social Stories

Writing is no easy task – trust me! We often worry that we are going to make a mistake and possibly do more harm than good. Don't worry too much and don't let this put you off creating your own social stories. First off, I am going to give you a social story that I have adapted for different ages, so you can see the level of language, detail, and vocabulary to use.

For the toddler story, I have also created a comic strip conversation. It's very simplified but it really doesn't have to be complicated. I would add colour, though. You are more than welcome to use my ideas and make little changes so that it is more personal.

Social Stories and Comic Strip Conversations for Anger

For Toddlers

'Sometimes I feel angry. When I am angry, I want to hit Mummy or throw my toys. This makes Mummy feel sad. I don't like it when Mummy feels sad. When I feel angry, I need to stop. I can hold my hands. I can breathe slowly. This makes me calm.'

When I Am Calm, Mummy Is Happy

So, each sentence should be on a separate page. You might be able to get photos of them when they are angry or of you feeling sad. You can also use emojis. A great image for the 'stop' page is a stop traffic sign or a big red hand with the palm facing you.

For Children

'I have a lot of feelings. Some of my feelings make me feel good and others make me feel bad. When I feel angry, I feel bad. Sometimes, my friends make me angry. Sometimes, my teacher makes me angry. Other times, my family can make me angry. The problem is, when I am angry, I want to shout or hit the other person. But if I shout at the other person, I can make them feel sad or even angry. If I hit or kick the other person, I could hurt them as well as make them feel sad or angry. Instead, I have to practise being calm.

To help me feel calm, I could sit down and breathe while I count to 10. I could also play with a fidget toy or a ball. I could jump up and down or run around. When I feel calm, I can talk to the other person and explain why I was angry. I will try hard to use nice words so that we both feel better.'

You can see that the older the child gets, the more important it is to adapt the story. In this case, you might notice that rather than being an outlet for anger, physical activities make your child more energetic, or 'hyped up', in which case you would need to change this activity for something that works for them. Instead of a fidget toy, you might notice that stroking the family pet calms them down.

Below is a comic strip conversation for toddlers based on the social story:

There are apps that will allow you to create comic strips but if you are anything like me, they will take far longer than simple drawing by hand. The point of using stick figures is so the attention remains on the conversation, rather than the drawings.

15 Social Stories You Can Adapt

First Day of Nursery

'Soon, I am going to start nursery. I am a little bit scared but I'm also excited. I will give Mummy and Daddy a kiss goodbye. It's okay to feel sad. I will meet my teacher. I will make new friends. I will play with lots of toys. My teacher will read stories. It will be lots of fun. Mummy and Daddy will pick me up and I can tell them about my day.'

First Day of School

'Soon, I am starting school. I have my new school bag and pencil case. I must take care of my things. Mummy and Daddy will drive me to school. First, we will wait at the gate and when my teacher comes out, I will say goodbye to Mummy and Daddy. In my classroom, I will find my place and sit down with my new friends. I will listen carefully to the teacher and raise my hand if I need help. During the break, I will play nicely with my friends and take turns. When school finishes, I will put my things away and take my school bag. Mummy and Daddy will be there to pick me up. After a hug and a kiss, I can tell them about my day.'

A Visit to the Doctor

'I have a check-up with the doctor. I will go to the doctor with Granny because Daddy is at work. When we arrive, Granny will say hello to the receptionist and I will tell them my name. We will sit down and wait. I'm a little bit nervous, so I ask Granny if I can hold her hand. The doctor will call my name and we go to her room. There are lots of posters on the wall. I like the one with animals. The doctor asks me what my favourite animal is and I start to feel more relaxed. The doctor will check my eyes, ears, and mouth. I will stand on the scales to see how much I weigh and she measures my height. She will ask me about what I like to eat and if I like to sleep. Finally, I will need an injection. I might be scared but I will hold Granny's hand again. After the doctor's, Granny will take me to the park and we will play.'

For the doctors and dentist, it is particularly useful if you can get some photos of the waiting room and the doctor or dentist beforehand. Be sure to ask and explain why you need the photos. Also, having photos of older siblings having their vaccinations can really help.

My First School Trip

Most children are excited about getting out of the classroom but this is a break from the routine and there will be plenty of new situations they have to face. If you notice that your little one is nervous in new environments, this can help a lot.

'My class is going on a school trip. We are going to a wildlife park. First, we will go on a bus. When we arrive, we have to line up and wait to enter. Inside the wildlife park, we will see lots of animals. Some animals will be big and others will be small. We have to be quiet so we don't scare the animals. In our backpacks, we have our lunch. I will eat with my friends at picnic tables. I have to throw all of my rubbish in the bin. After lunch, we will see more animals and some plants. The bus will take us back to school and Mummy and Daddy will pick me up.'

My Friend Is Autistic

'My friend is autistic. They have some problems that I don't. Sometimes, they find it hard to talk to me. There are some days when they can't stop tapping the table. Other days they get very angry and upset with different people. It's important that I am a good friend. I can be a good friend by not laughing and by asking them what they need. I can respect them when they don't want to talk. I can use kind words to show I care. If other children aren't kind to my friend, I can tell a teacher. By trying to understand how my friend feels, I can be a good friend.'

Of course, this type of social story is very specific. It can be adapted to any friend who may be considered different from other children in the class. The goal of this type of story will be understanding diversity, respecting different children's needs, and a hope to reduce bullying.

My Table Manners

'Before I eat breakfast, lunch, or dinner, I have to wash my hands. I ask Mummy or Daddy if I can help. I sit at the table and wait patiently for my food. I say thank you. When everybody has their food, I can use my knife and fork to eat. I take small bites so that I can close my mouth when I'm eating. If I accidentally spill my drink or my food, I say sorry and wipe it up. After everyone has finished their meal, I take my plate to the kitchen sink.'

Parent's Divorce

'My Mummy and Daddy love me very much. They also love each other. But they argue a lot and this makes them very sad. My parents are going to get a divorce. Mummy will have one house and Daddy will have another. Sometimes I will stay at Mummy's house. Other times, I will stay at Daddy's house. It isn't my fault and it's not because they don't love me. They want to be very good friends so that they can both be happy. When my parents are happy, I can be happy.'

My New Hobby

'Soon, I am going to start swimming lessons. I will go to the swimming pool every Saturday morning at 10 o'clock. I need to take my swimsuit, a towel, and my swimming goggles. I will shower before I get into the swimming pool. My teacher will help me learn how to swim. I have to listen carefully. If I am scared, I can tell my teacher and they will help me. If I don't feel safe, I can also tell my teacher. I will meet new friends. Together, we will have fun. After my swimming lesson, I will have a shower, get dressed, and brush my hair.'

My New Sibling

'Mummy has a baby in her tummy. It's my brother or sister. Soon, she will go to the hospital and have the baby. I will miss her but I will be brave because when she comes home, she will have my new baby brother or sister. I have to be careful with the baby because he or she will be very small. Mummy and Daddy will help me give him or her cuddles. Sometimes, Mummy and Daddy will have to take care of the baby. If this makes me sad or upset, I will tell Mummy and Daddy how I feel. At first, it might be difficult for me. But Mummy, Daddy, and my brother or sister love me and we will have new adventures together.'

My First Sleepover

'Jimmy is my best friend. Soon, I am going to his house for a sleepover. After school, his dad will pick us up and take us home to his house. We will get changed and go and play. The rules at Jimmy's house might be different from mine. I must listen carefully to the rules so that we can have fun. At dinner time, we will eat together. I have to be polite and remember my manners. Sleeping in Jimmy's room will also be different. I will remember the fun we had and not be scared. The next day, after breakfast, Jimmy's mum will take us to school. I must remember to say thank you to Jimmy's mum.'

Going to a Birthday Party

'It's Sally's birthday and she is having a party. I will wear a special dress. The party starts at 5 o'clock. I can't be late because that is rude. I will give Sally a present. I might feel jealous because Sally is getting lots of new toys. But I will remember that it is her special day and this makes me happy. We will play some games. If I don't win, that will be ok, as long as we have fun. Sally's family will bring in a big cake and we will all sing happy birthday. When the party finishes, I will give Sally a big hug, say happy birthday again and go home.'

Taking Turns

'When I play with my friends or my family, I have to take turns. Sometimes I don't like this. I want to have another turn because I think it's not fair. When people say I can't have a turn, I get angry and I don't want to play. This makes me sad because then nobody wants to play. I have to think about how I would feel if my friends or family wouldn't let me take turns. I need to take some deep breaths to feel calm while the other person has their turn. I can be a good team player by encouraging them. Soon, it will be my turn again.'

Making Friends

'I can make friends at school. Or at the park. Or at my after-school activities. I can ask people if they would like to talk or play with me. I will use kind words and ask nicely. Sometimes they will say yes. Other times, they will say no. This is okay. My friends will all be different. Some will be tall and some will be short. Some will be good at math and others good at football. We should all respect our differences. Even when I have friends, I should keep making new friends, especially if I see someone who finds it hard to make friends.'

Potty Training

'Now that I am a big girl, I am going to start using the potty. When I need to go to the bathroom, I will tell

Mummy or Daddy. I will pull down my trousers and knickers and sit on the potty. Sometimes, I will have to wait. I can sing a song or read a story. When I have finished, I will wipe my bottom. I will pull up my knickers and trousers. Mummy or Daddy will help me empty the potty. Then we will wash our hands. Mummy and Daddy will give me a sticker for my great job.'

Transitioning

Transitioning is a crucial skill that allows children to transition from one activity to another. You might notice that at home, children will start with one game or toy, move on to the next, and then the next. In no time, your living room has every single toy spread across the floor. Once in a while, this is ok, if they are going to tidy it all up.

Imagine if as an adult, you were unable to transition from one task to another. You would literally be taking half of your dirty laundry to work, the dinner would be half-cooked, and so on. Children need to learn how to complete one activity before moving on to the next. This will be an asset for them at school. This story will be related to playing, but you can create a social story about any activity where they need to complete one activity before another (getting fully dressed before cleaning teeth, for example).

'I love playing with my blocks. There are different shapes and colours. I can make different things with my bricks. When I have finished playing with my bricks, I have to put all my bricks away because I don't want to lose any. If I put all my bricks away, the next time I play, I will have all of my bricks to build more things. When all of my bricks are tidied away, I can choose another toy.'

As an end to this chapter, please don't take my reference to Mum and Dad as prescriptive or old-fashioned or biased in any way. In my line of work, I am well aware of the multiple family dynamics. If I started creating social stories for all types of caregivers you would be reading for a long time! This is another reason why you should create your own or adapt these so that you can insert the person who picks them up from school or takes them to the dentist.

Print off your social stories and to make them last longer, laminate them and use ring binders to make a little book. Save them all in a box so that you can easily access them and read them on regular occasions before a new situation comes up.

Chapter 12: Walk a Mile in the Parents' Shoes

You might have already seen how we walked a mile in the child's shoes in my previous book. To become more empathetic, it's important to try and see things from their point of view. Nevertheless, you also need to know that you are not alone.

This chapter is dedicated to all of you amazing parents who are tirelessly striving to make life better for your children. Here are some stories that people have shared with me and I think it helps far more than people giving you advice like 'It could be worse' and 'Look on the bright side'.

The Inspirational Julie

We are going to start with my dear friend Julie Pharo, who some of you may have seen in the group. She certainly had an interesting start in the world of speech and language therapy. Although she is amazing at her job, it's her personal story that touched my heart and I think many of you will relate to it.

Julie's son, Aron, is now 23. He finished school, has a job, and drives himself to work. But the future wasn't all that clear for Aron. At Aron's eight-week check-up, the doctors told Julie that he was deaf. At the time, Julie felt a huge amount of grief. As mums, we spend almost nine months panicking that our babies aren't going to be healthy, or there will be some kind of problem. When your baby is born, and you discover that life isn't going to be as easy for your little one, there is a sense of grief for that easier life.

Unless you are in this kind of situation where your child needs additional support, you won't understand this, and that's ok. And yes, there are women who miscarry, and babies who don't survive more than a few weeks or months, and that is tragic. But that doesn't mean that you aren't allowed to take a moment to process your feelings, whether that's anger at the world, grief, sadness, etc. – you have every right to feel the way you do. Your child needs you on your top game and burying your emotions is likely to make your suffering worse.

So, back to Julie. After a hospital appointment that confirmed Aron was deaf, Julie was at a complete loss. The advice she got was to google information on Makaton. After a trip to the library, and the librarian having to google what Makaton was, Julie was told that they would have to order the books in. That was the support 23 years ago. Julie taught herself Makaton, and by the age of one, Aron began signing his basic needs.

At school, Aron had no support. There were no SEN teachers or assistants, no hearing aids, and compared with today, there was no support. Today, there is so much more support for all the different types of social delays and disorders, but you still might feel like you are in Julie's shoes because there is a significant wait.

Aron's success throughout primary and secondary school as well as into adult life has so much to do with the research and influence Julie and her family had at home. Julie had no speech and language background, and she worked a few evening shifts at Tesco. She could have accepted what the doctors said, that he was deaf and that was it. But she took it on herself to make Aron's life better.

This is an inspiration for all parents. It doesn't matter how old you are or what your background is. It doesn't matter about your level of education. You can make a difference too. Maybe you aren't reading this book for your own child. Perhaps, like Julie, you are taking it into the classroom. Or you are trying to support a friend or relative with a child that needs additional support. Know that you are making a difference too.

What It's Like Raising a Child With ASD

The name itself tells us that there is a huge spectrum to consider – parents will have different experiences to share. But one of my favourite stories was how a mum compared being a parent to being at secondary school. This I can seriously relate to. Moving to the UK as a young teenager and starting secondary school with no English is something I will never forget. There are the cool kids, the 'nerds', and then the 'different kids'.

As the parent of a child with ASD, it's like walking down the corridor and the cool kids are looking at you with pity or embarrassment. This shouldn't bother you – but it does. It's not so much because you want to fit in with the cool parents, but you want your child to make friends with the cool parents' kids... or any kids. And this is what can hurt.

The meltdowns can be the worst. You can see them coming – heck, you can feel them coming. And you know that regardless of what you do, your child is going to suffer. Seeing the tears running down their face is enough to tear your heart in two. When you are exhausted, stressed, and possibly under the watchful eye of judgemental parents, it's hard to remain empathetic and it's hard not to want to curl up in your own mini-meltdown.

Part of my job is also to support parents and one of the things I always say to parents, whether it's ASD or other early social interaction challenges, is that you have to take care of yourself and in particular, your stress levels.

Did you know that mothers who take care of autistic children experience the same levels of chronic stress as soldiers in combat (Journal of Autism and Developmental Disorders, n.d.)? Naturally, this is because you want to dedicate as much of your energy towards helping your child as you can. I hope that the games and activities in this book will provide some moments of reduced stress and enjoyment for you and your family.

Children with Social Anxiety Disorder

Words like 'confusing' and 'frustrating' often pop up when talking to parents whose children have social anxiety. It's often hard for them to understand why their little one can have a full-on conversation with some people and then completely freeze with others. Or why they seem shy in the classroom but refuse to mix with others at a birthday party with the same friends.

The Internet is a great source of information but, any parent who googles the cause of social anxiety will often feel like they are to blame. Social anxiety is often caused by environmental factors. This could imply stress in their early years or family history, but it can also arise from bullying or teasing at school.

It was interesting to talk to one mum who had a very sociable one-year-old. She taught private classes out of her home, so her little one was used to having plenty of people around. After three months of lockdown during the pandemic, her little one would cry as soon as she saw anyone in the street. Because little people are often too young to explain their emotions to us, or are not quite aware of them themselves, it is hard for us to know what is causing them to fear social situations.

From a parent's point of view, it seems like a lack of self-esteem and/or confidence. And this is true, but these are traits that we can't force anyone into having more of. Many parents feel that if they could just give their child a gentle push, they would overcome their fear, talk to a friend, and gain more confidence. One dad I spoke to thought this was the right approach (and believe me, it's not only dads!). Parents have tried bribes, threats, even begging, but they haven't been able to take a step back and see that their child *can't* talk to certain people, rather than *won't*.

The games that you should focus on are those that improve their confidence in social situations that they already feel confident in. So, activities that promote problem-solving within the family can help. Pay attention to the friends they talk about in school and invite them to playdates. Look for activities that offer opportunities to socialise but are extremely appealing to them. This might not be the traditional team activities but things like robotics or chess clubs.

There are lots of ways a child can lack early interaction skills and these can appear at different milestones. Reach out for support, not only for your child but also for you. It could be online forums, a friend who will actively listen rather than try to bombard you with advice, or a therapist if need be.

There is no harm in needing support while you are giving so much help to your child.

Conclusion

You have reached the end of what I hope is far more than just a book full of games and activities. I began with a little bit of a science lesson. Knowing that there is more than being socially comfortable and the fight or flight response will significantly help you to understand how adults and children react in certain ways.

Part of being good at social interactions is to be able to read body language and facial expressions. Our logical mind might see something one way, but long before this has happened, our brains have picked up on signs and are telling our nervous systems how to react. In the book, I covered examples of this between adults and children. But so you can see how crucial this is as the first stage of communication, let's look at a situation you have probably all been in at least one moment of your life.

Your partner walks in the door. Dinner is nearly ready and you are just about to do the usual 'How was your day' when you see the hint of a frown. Before you know it, your body has taken over, your mouth seems out of control and instead of asking if they are ok, there is a hint of anger as you say, 'What's wrong with you?'.

When you take a step back and look at how your nervous system reacts, it becomes so much easier to see why your child may react the way they do, even if it seems completely out of the blue.

I know there was a fair amount of promoting early on in the book. I can't help it. I'm so excited about my programme because it has been specifically created so that I can help more people but in an individual way. Having to wait for diagnoses and referrals is exasperating and infuriating. This programme will help parents get support as soon as possible. Plus, you can find loads of freebies and support on the Facebook community, so I would love to see you there.

This is the last time I'll say it, I promise! Milestones are a guideline; some will be hit before and others later. You have amazing instincts, so if you feel like something isn't quite right, see your doctor or bring up your concerns during check-ups and revisions. If other parents have reverted back to the competitiveness of secondary school, leave them be! You have better things to do with your time.

Like, for example, playing one of the 137 [JM4]games and activities in this book. Busy parents need quick references to find the information they need. For this reason, each chapter is split into age groups. If you are feeling a bit stressed and panicked, you can flip open the chapter you need and start straight away.

I recommend trying to go back and read over the other chapters when you have time. This is because all of the games can be adapted for different age groups. The other advantage of going over all of the ideas is that you can make a list of the activities you want to try and start collecting some of the materials you need. Nothing has to cost a fortune. Toilet roll holders have probably never appeared more valuable than they have after looking at mini-mes, animals, and characters for pretend play.

It's almost an impossible task, but if I had to choose a handful of my favourite games and activities, I would choose:

- The Treasure Path
- Blowing Bubbles
- Pretend Play
- Cooking
- The Emotion Thermometer
- Fill the Post Box
- Making Household Chores a Game
- Draw Your Emotions
- The Family Contest
- Watch Bluey
- Lego Therapy
- It's Your Turn
- Lily Pad Sight Words

First of all, I have developed a new and recent love for the cartoon *Bluey*. There is something so simple about the content. Aside from teaching children important social skills, it will also help them learn how to talk about their feelings. What's more, it's a great (and humorous) reminder to parents that you just need to slow down and enjoy this time with your children. Plus, as it's unlikely that you can completely avoid the TV, at least you can make sure they are getting the most out of it.

Things like blowing bubbles and lily pad sight words, along with reading the books I have listed in each chapter, are really going to help with speech and language development. This is the cornerstone of communication and will help build their confidence.

Emotional awareness is invaluable. Society is getting better but there is a long way before we can say that all emotions are equally valid. The fact is that no emotion is good or bad. They are there for a purpose and children need to get good at learning what that purpose is. When they get better at labelling these emotions, they will understand that it's the behaviour that is good or bad, not the emotion. This is why I love drawing emotions and especially the emotion thermometer.

Pretend play is awesome for creativity, role play, and seeing things from different points of view. To take that a step further, you and your little one can do activities like cooking and cleaning together. It's not slave labour! These activities can be extremely fun and help to improve listening and following instructions.

Housework and taking care of plants and pets teach responsibility. Even young children can understand accountability, even if they can't explain exactly what it means. This skill is highly transferable. As older children, they will learn that they have to be accountable for their studies and how they treat their friends.

I can't believe I included a comic strip conversation, and please, feel free to laugh at my drawings. Also, know that your stick figures can't be any worse than mine, so you are more than capable of creating your own.

You are the best person to write social stories because you know exactly what your child is going to find upsetting or terrifying. You can incorporate real characters that will provide some safety and reassurance. And if you can add photos, these visual images are going to add to the benefits. When it comes to comic strip conversations, you are also the best person to predict just what answer they will have!

When you are creating comic strips, conversations, or social stories, remember to keep the focus on the positive solutions and outcomes rather than the negative behaviours. Naturally, you need to include the goal that you want to overcome, but the focus will always be the process of solving potential problems.

You can use your own social stories the same way you may have used other books. So when they are confident with the story, you can choose to not turn the page but instead, ask them what happens next. Or put forward a different scenario and see how they would end the story.

Your goal is five minutes a day. Five minutes with absolutely no distractions. Little siblings can be taking a nap, older siblings can be doing their homework. There are no phones or TV. More and more children are feeling that they come second to a parent's mobile phone. From your point of view, you are using strategic playtime to boost early interaction skills. From their point of view, they just see one of the most important people in their lives wanting to spend special time with them. Nothing is more important than that!

After those five minutes, well, that's a bit of a free-for-all. Sometimes you won't be able to play for longer, but don't beat yourself up about that. Have a mad-dash half an hour and see if you can squeeze in another five minutes later. Other days, they won't be interested in playing more (of course, you know this will be the day you happen to have freed up more time!). Don't take it personally. Their attention spans are developing and there is still a lot going on in those little minds. Follow their lead.

The conclusion of any book is always the hardest for me. I have mixed emotions. I want to get it out as soon as possible but I also feel like I'm saying goodbye, which I know sounds silly. For this reason, I really hope I see so many of you on Facebook or via my website, so I can find out how things are going for you and if I can help in other ways.

Another way I love to hear from people is through Amazon. Reviews are essential, not for sales, but so that other parents who are in the same position as you can start making a difference in their children's lives as soon as possible. I thank you in advance if you can leave a quick review!

http://mybook.to/SLT4Toddlers

Until then, good luck, and have faith in your own abilities as an amazing parent!

http://mybook.to/SLT4Toddlers

References

Daniels, E. (2017, September 23). Homemade Face Paint Recipe and Color Chart. Personal Creations Blog. Retrieved November 20, 2021, from https://www.personalcreations.com/blog/homemade-face-paint.

Diament, M. (2015, November 20). Autism Moms Have Stress Similar To Combat Soldiers. Disability Scoop. Retrieved November 20, 2021, from https://www.disabilityscoop.com/2009/11/10/autism-moms-stress/6121/.

Home of Dr. Stephen Porges. (n.d.), stephenporges.com. Retrieved November 20, 2021, from https://www.stephenporges.com/bio.

McMaster University (2012, May 9). Babies' brains benefit from music lessons, even before they can walk and talk. ScienceDaily. Retrieved November 20, 2021, from https://www.sciencedaily.com/releases/2012/05/120509123653.htm.

National Autistic Society (n.d.). Social stories and comic strip conversations. autism.org. Retrieved November 20, 2021, from https://www.autism.org.uk/advice-and-guidance/topics/communication/communication-tools/social-stories-and-comic-strip-coversations.

Nemours Kids Health (n.d.). Learning, Play, and Your 1- to 3-Month-Old (for Parents) - Nemours KidsHealth. kidshealth.org. Retrieved November 20, 2021, from https://kidshealth.org/en/parents/learn13m.html.

Nerd Nite. (2017, November 4). The Polyvagal Theory: The New Science of Safety and Trauma [Video]. YouTube. https://www.youtube.com/watch?v=br8-qebjIgs.

Pathways. (2019, August 22). Early Child Development Abilities by Age. pathways. org. Retrieved November 20, 2021, from https://pathways.org/all-ages/abilities/.

Rusmayadi, R., & Herman, H. (2019, August). Effects of Social Skills on Early Childhood Independence. Researchgate. Retrieved November 20, 2021, from https://www.researchgate.net/publication/336286188_Effects_of_Social_Skills_on_Early_Childhood_Independence.

Suttie, J. (2020, February 24). Kids Do Better on the Marshmallow Test When They Cooperate. Greater Good. Retrieved November 20, 2021, from https://greatergood.berkeley.edu/article/item/kids_do_better_on_the_marshmallow_test_when_they_cooperate.

University of Oregon Center on Teaching and Learning (n.d.). Vocabulary: Concepts and Research. reading.uoregon.edu. Retrieved November 20, 2021, from http://reading.uoregon.edu/big_ideas/voc/voc_what.php.

Weitzman, E. (n.d.). Why Interaction Must Come Before Language. hanen.org. Retrieved November 20, 2021, from http://www.hanen.org/Helpful-Info/Articles/Why-Interaction-Must-Come-Before-Language.aspx.

Manufactured by Amazon.ca
Bolton, ON

44319518R10098